Coping with

MELANOMA AND OTHER SKIN CANCERS

Wendy Long

THE ROSEN PUBLISHING GROUP, INC./NEW YORK

This book is dedicated to a physician I know. His compassion and intelligence inspire awe in me and in his patients. He only does one thing better than being a doctor, and that's being my dad. Thank you for the constant support.

Published in 1999 by The Rosen Publishing Group, Inc.
29 East 21st Street, New York, NY 10010

First Edition

Cover photograph by Brian T. Silak

Library of Congress Cataloging-in-Publication Data

Long, Wendy, 1958–
   Coping with melanoma and other skin cancers / Wendy Long.
     p.   cm.
   Includes bibliographical references and index.
   Summary: Explains the causes and treatment of melanoma and other skin cancers, including detection, prevention, and coping techniques.
   ISBN 0-8239-2852-7
   1. Melanoma—Juvenile literature. 2. Skin—Cancer—Juvenile litera-
ture. [1. Melanoma. 2. Skin—Cancer. 3. Cancer. 4. Diseases.] I. Title
   RC280.M37L66 1999
   616.99'477'dc21   99-36223
                                                       CIP
                                                           AC

Manufactured in the United States of America

About the Author

Wendy Long is a medical student and writer living in New York City.

Contents

Introduction

It Can't Be Skin Cancer! I Never Go in the Sun!

"I always stay out of the sun! It can't possibly be skin cancer," remarked Allison. Allison's friend Jessica had told her she should get a mole on her arm checked out by a dermatologist. Jessica was concerned about Allison's mole because it had changed size and color over the past few months. Although exposure to the sun is a risk factor for skin cancer, it is not the only one. Allison should take Jessica's advice. The earlier a doctor properly diagnoses skin cancer, the better.

Skin, the Sun, and Cancer

Your skin is the largest organ of your body. In recent years, you may have heard a lot about skin cancer. In the United States, the rate of skin cancer has been rising rapidly, faster than many other kinds of cancers. Maybe your parents told you to use SPF 15 sunblock when you wanted to get a nice tan. Many cosmetic companies have developed new tanning lotions that allow you to get a ruddy glow without "baking" in the sun. But just like many people spend a lot of time in the sun without developing skin cancer, not

1

everyone who gets skin cancer has spent too much time in the sun.

So how come everyone seems to tell you that if you stay out of the sun, then you will not get skin cancer? There are actually many risk factors involved in skin cancer. The single biggest risk factor is ignorance. Many people, doctors included, used to believe that the ultraviolet (UV) radiation of sunlight was a major cause of skin cancer. But sunlight actually only increases the likelihood that a person will get a skin cancer, such as melanoma, by two to four times.

Other risk factors are much more significant. A mole like Allison's, which has changed size or color, can increase the likelihood of a person developing melanoma by up to 400 times. So by giving almost exclusive attention to the danger of the sun, many parents, doctors, and members of the media have put the public at a disadvantage. Yes, exposure to direct sunlight can be dangerous, but people also need to be aware of the many other risk factors for skin cancer. The ignorance surrounding this lethal cancer of the largest organ of the body needs to be replaced by a common knowledge of skin cancer and its warning signs.

This is not to say that it is perfectly safe to get out the baby oil and hit the beach in search of the perfect tan. The sun does cause damage that leads to some kinds of skin cancer. However, everyone needs to understand that even if you stay out of the sun, you can still be at risk for skin cancer. Everyone should see a dermatologist at least once for an evaluation of his or her skin cancer risk and to make a lifelong screening plan. You will be much better equipped to prevent the development of skin cancer if you understand what your skin does, how it works, and the process of cancer.

Your skin is your largest organ, but unlike other organs, you can see most of it. Your ability to see your skin is your best defense against developing a skin cancer that could be life-threatening. Understanding your skin, what is normal and what is not, and understanding the stages of development of skin cancer enables you to know when it is the right time to go to a dermatologist. The earlier a doctor finds a skin cancer or a skin "growth" that may become cancerous, the better.

What does "better" mean? It means having a smaller scar, if any scar at all, after the growth is removed. It means fewer visits to the doctor. It means less money spent on treatment. It could mean a better chance to live.

So you already know that staying out of the sun or wearing at least SPF 15 sunblock is a good idea. Now you need to know about your skin and about skin cancer. Allison is lucky that her friend Jessica knew enough to tell her to go to a doctor. But not everyone has friends or family that know enough about skin cancer to help in that way.

If you understand skin cancer and its risk factors, then you will be able to examine yourself. In addition to taking care of yourself, you will be able to help others that you care about—friends or family members—just like Jessica helped Allison.

The more that people know about skin cancer and its risk factors, the fewer people will die from this disease. You can start to work to decrease the mortality (death) rates from skin cancer by simply reading this book and using some of the educational resources listed in the back. You can educate yourself and teach others to do the same thing. Doesn't it feel good to know that you are helping to defeat a deadly disease?

Understanding Your Skin

Skin seems pretty simple. Well, it is basically simple. The most important thing to remember about skin, especially in respect to cancer, is that it is made up of several different layers of cells. These layers are continuous around your body. Some layers become thicker or thinner in certain places where the skin serves slightly different functions.

For example, the outermost layer of skin is made up of dead skin cells. This layer is thickest on the bottom of your feet because your skin here becomes toughened as you walk, run, dance, stand, and move about. The skin of your eyelids is much different, as you can easily tell. This skin functions as protection for the delicate eye tissue, and is involved in very fine and precise movements such as winking. While the skin's layers may change in thickness, they are all present at all points in the skin on the exposed surface of your body.

Layers of the Epidermis

Your skin is made up of different but not totally separate structural layers—the epidermis, the basement membrane, and the dermis. When people talk about the skin, they are generally referring to the epidermis, which is the outermost part of the skin that you can see and touch. The epidermis is where skin cancer most often begins. The epidermis itself is made up of several layers of cells that are continuous and connected. Each layer contains specific cell types. The most common kind of skin cells are called keratinocytes.

The innermost layer of the epidermis, the basal layer, is made up of cells with the ability to divide and develop into the different cell types of the next layer. You can think of the basal layer as the place where the cells of the skin are created. As each cell matures, it moves outward from layer to layer. The function and structure of each cell changes as it matures and moves out.

The layer next to the basal layer is the spindle layer. Under a microscope, the cells of this layer look as though they have spindles or spines. These cells are tightly stuck together (adherent) due to special attachment bridges. The plasticity, or resilience, of your skin is largely due to this layer, which is helped by the supportive tissues that lie underneath the epidermis. As a result, the skin can be pushed and pulled and stretched in daily activity without splitting open. This is because the cells of the spindle layer stick to one another and change shape under force but do not let go of the cells next to them.

There is a pattern to a cell's journey from the innermost to the outermost layer. A skin cell is born at the base and develops as it moves outward. Eventually, as it reaches the outermost layer, it dies. After the spindle layer, the cell begins to die. Its nucleus, which contains the cell's DNA, begins to disintegrate. At this point, these cells make up what is known as the granular layer, because the disintegrating DNA material makes the cells look granular or grainy.

Eventually, by the time the cell dies, it has reached the outermost layer, which is known as the keratinized, squamous layer or the cornified layer. These cells are anucleate (without a nucleus) because they lost their nuclei in the granular layer. Under a microscope, they look like ghosts, because they have lost most of the internal cell structures of a living cell.

The dead cells of this layer mostly contain keratin, a protein that is common throughout the skin. This layer is what keeps you watertight, so that you don't soak up water like a sponge when you get in the tub or dry out when at the beach on a hot day.

This is also the layer that changes thickness the most from one part of your body to the next. The keratinized, squamous layer is thin on the inside of your elbow, but very thick on the bottom of your foot. This makes a difference in everyday activity. It would be pretty painful to walk if your feet were not protected by thick skin. Imagine trying to wink at someone if your eyelids were as thick as the calluses on your big toe. The thickness of the outer dead layer of skin cells changes normally depending on where it is on the body and with age. Your skin naturally becomes thinner as you get older. However, skin thickness can also change abnormally with certain types of cancer.

So at the base of the epidermis there is the basal layer, then the sticky, spindle layer, the grainy, granular layer, and the ghostly, dead, keratinized, squamous layer. Most cancers of the skin involve the cells known as the keratinocytes, but there are three other types of cells in your epidermis that are important and can also be involved in cancers—the melanocyte, the Langerhans cell, and the Merkel cell. Melanocytes produce melanin, which is a pigment in the epidermis that allows humans to have a huge spectrum of different skin colors—sandy red, tawny brown, dark chocolate, creamy white, ebony. Melanin also causes people of most colors to "tan" from sun exposure. Why do humans need skin color at all? What biological purpose does melanin serve? The melanin produced by the melanocytes is used by other cells to shield their nuclei from the sun. Melanin serves as a kind of natural sunscreen.

The ultraviolet (UV) radiation of the sun's rays damages the DNA in skin cells. Such damage does not always create problems, and the cell can continue to divide and make its journey from the base until it dies naturally.

However, too much accumulated damage to the DNA of skin cells causes cancer. The more sun bathing you do, the more likely you are to get skin cancer. Melanin is what the skin uses to shield its DNA naturally from UV radiation. When a person with a light complexion goes outside, the sun's rays will promote the production of melanin by the melanocytes. When you get a tan, your skin has actually made its own anti-radiation suit. However, melanin does not provide total protection from the damaging effect of UV radiation, which is why you need to use sunscreen. Sunscreen helps the body's natural protection, melanin, to protect your skin.

There are two other kinds of skin cells in the epidermis. The Langerhans cell is a rare cell that is involved in immune defense, which is the process the body uses to protect itself against outside agents, especially bacteria, viruses, and other organisms that cause disease. In a way, the skin is the first line of this defense, since it is the place where outside organisms and particles first interact with your body. The Merkel cell is what is known as a mechanoreceptor, which is a structure that allows your skin to feel mechanical force or pressure from an outside agent.

Support for the Epidermis

The epidermis lies on a basement membrane that serves as a foundation for the layers. The basement membrane is made up of cells and fibrous proteins that act as a support, or foundation, for the epidermis. It also acts as a filter to allow specific cells and nutrients to flow freely from the underlying dermis. The dermis is made up of fibers and immune system cells and contains the rich nerve and blood supply that the epidermis needs.

You can think of the epidermis as a building with four stories—the basal, spindle, granular, and keratinized, squamous layers. The basement membrane is the foundation for the building. The dermis is what lies underneath the building—pipes containing nutrients and the deep, underground support beams that keep the building stable.

Malignant
Melanoma

The human body is made up of cells. The cells in the body do not live a random, unorganized life. Each cell has a specific life span. Imagine if all the cells in the body grew and divided continuously and none of them ever died. We would all look like Jabba the Hut in no time at all.

Each cell has a "script" that details the role the cell plays throughout its life. For example, this "script" tells the cell when to divide and when to die. The life and activity of a cell are tightly regulated by the cell's genome, which is the collection of DNA genes in the cell's nucleus. The genome contains the pre-written script or code for the cell's role and function in the body. The genome controls how long the cell lives, how many times it will divide and form other cells of its type, and all the other functions it performs, such as producing melanin, for example. If the DNA of the genome is damaged, the cell's script is rewritten, changed, or mutated.

A mutation means that genes have been passed on from one cell to the next with an incorrect pattern or code. A mutation can delete whole sections of DNA. Sometimes the DNA is damaged in such a way that the mutation causes parts of the script to repeat itself. When the cell divides, its "daughter cells" have two copies of a specific gene instead of one. Damage to DNA can be very subtle, involving a switch or deletion of only one letter at one point in the script. In certain instances, the cell can still read what it is supposed to do if a letter is different or missing. These little mutations or deletions can add up, though.

This often happens when UV radiation damages the DNA of skin cells.

UV radiation causes a specific mutation in the DNA of skin cells. It causes a specific base, or molecule, that makes up DNA to pair up, or dimerize. These dimeric photoproducts change the shape and therefore the "script" or code of the mutated DNA.

There is a repair system in all of your cells that makes sure mutations are fixed before the cell replicates and passes the mutation on to its two daughter cells. In some individuals, though, this repair system does not work right. These people are more likely to develop cancer.

At first, these small mutations do not change the way the cell works. However, after enough time in the sun without adequate sunscreen, the mutations accumulate and can result in the development of specific skin cancers.

When enough DNA damage accumulates, a cell exists that has lost some of the genes that tell it to stop dividing and to die. The genes that tell the cell to die have been damaged.

The result is a cell in the skin that continues to divide forever. The mutations in this cell have affected other functions besides its ability to know when to initiate its natural death process, which is called apoptosis. It is a cell that is both abnormal and immortal. It continues to divide over and over again, without stopping. Its daughter cells are also abnormal and immortal. A population of abnormal cells in the skin is a tumor or skin cancer.

Cancer, then, is simply the unchecked reproduction of abnormal cells in some part of the body. After some period of time, a tumor forms, and the cancer cells in the epidermis, for example, can break through their natural and normal boundary, the basement membrane. These cells can continue to divide in the dermis, even though that is not their normal habitat. They can also get into blood vessels, or lymph vessels, and travel to other parts of the body. In this way, cancer cells can travel to the lungs, the liver, or the brain and create a new tumor that damages and kills the surrounding normal tissue. This is the next stage of a cancer and is known as metastasis.

There is a particular vocabulary that people use to categorize cancer types. Cancer of the tissue that lines the outside and inside of your body, the epithelium, is called carcinoma. Skin is an epithelium, so skin cancer falls under the category of a carcinoma.

What does skin cancer look like? Are there different kinds? Can you get treatment for skin cancer or, even better yet, prevent it? In order to answer these questions, you have to look at your skin and get used to what is normal and healthy.

Freckles, Moles, and Birthmarks

As you can see by looking around, not everyone's skin is the same. Skin color varies greatly. People also have other markings on their skin that make them unique. Some have freckles or birthmarks or lots of moles. Some people, known as albinos, have no color in their skin at all. Are all of these skin types normal and healthy? Are you more likely to get skin cancer if you freckle easily or if you have lots of moles?

First, let's talk about freckles, which are those flat little tan spots that generally show up on lighter-skinned people, especially those with red hair. Freckles are simply a place on the skin where the melanocytes are overproducing melanin. The sun induces freckles to come out, and they often disappear in the absence of sun, such as during the winter in a cold climate.

Freckles are totally normal and harmless. So are lentigos. Lentigos look very similar to freckles, but they are often darker and hang around all year long. Lentigos are small patches of skin that have more melanocytes. Lentigos are very common on the shoulders of men, who are more likely to spend time in the sun without wearing shirts. Generally, lentigos are harmless too. But although freckles and lentigos are not dangerous by themselves, they do indicate skin that has been irradiated by the sun, which can be very dangerous.

Now what about moles? Many people have moles on their skin. The medical term for a mole is a melanocytic nevus. Some people have moles at birth or get them while they are toddlers. These are known as congenital nevi. ("Nevi" is the plural for "nevus".) Other people develop moles into their thirties. These are known as acquired nevi.

Congenital nevi are often referred to as birthmarks. They are usually about 5 to 10 millimeters across, which is slightly wider than a pencil eraser. The smaller congenital nevi are found on 1 out of 100 newborns. Sometimes a child has a giant garment nevus, so called because it is

13

large enough to cover a child's abdomen and upper legs, like a big shirt. Small congenital nevi are not yet considered risk factors for skin cancer, but a child with a giant garment nevus has up to a 10 percent chance of developing skin cancer during her or his lifetime. Although it is difficult to remove an entire giant nevus surgically, this procedure usually is called for because of the increased cancer risk this kind of congenital nevi presents. People born with a giant garment nevus should be regularly checked for cancerous growth throughout their lives.

Acquired nevi, which are commonly referred to as moles, usually start appearing on a person at about the age of twelve. There are many different kinds of moles—flat or raised, red or brown or even blue in color. One kind of mole, called nevus "en cocarde," looks like a little rose or flower.

The human skin is capable of producing all of these different patterns and even some others. In and of themselves, none of these are necessarily harmful or dangerous. However, some people have many moles, even hundreds of them. This puts these people at increased risk for certain skin cancers. A normal, everyday mole, just like the one someone you know is bound to have on his or her back or arm, can become dangerous. If they change shape or color, moles may indicate the potential for cancerous development. Such moles are said to have become atypical nevi.

It is extremely important to know that nevi (moles) that start out normal can change—their shape, their color, or their borders. Routine self-examinations of the skin enable you to detect such changes easily if and when they occur. The ability to examine your own skin for irregular moles or other growths is your best defense against skin cancer.

The best prevention plan would combine an initial visit to a dermatologist for a skin check with your own monthly self-examinations. Your knowledge, and the ability to apply it, can save your own or maybe even someone else's life. A daily self-examination takes no more than a few moments.

Lynne

It was a bright, sunny day in August, and Lynne, Daniel, and Sara were on their way to the airport. They were flying to Europe to go backpacking for a few weeks. All the way there, they were joking and laughing in the back seat of the taxi that was taking them to their flight. When Lynne put her feet up on the back of the passenger seat, Sara, who was sitting next to her, noticed a strange-looking growth on Lynne's shin.

"Check that out, on your leg," Sara said as she pointed to Lynne's leg.

"Yeah," Lynne responded, with a roll of her eyes, "a weird, ugly mole."

"Well, I think you should get it checked out by a dermatologist. It looks kind of funky to me, like skin cancer, maybe," Sara noted.

"Sure, I'll just go back home and make an appointment right now!"

"No dummy! I mean after Europe," Sara replied, laughing.

The three of them had a great time in Europe. When they got back, Sara reminded Lynne about her mole. She went in to see a dermatologist to have it checked, and it did turn out to be a skin cancer in its early stages. Needless to say, Lynne thanked Sara.

Lynne's story demonstrates how important and powerful education about skin cancer can be. Sara had learned a bit about skin self-exams because she burned easily in the sun, and her doctor told her she could be at risk for skin cancer caused by sun damage. She never had a problem herself, but her knowledge allowed her to see a strange growth, which turned out to be cancerous, on her friend.

Lynne, by the way, was only nineteen at the time and is a dark-skinned person of Italian descent. Even people who are young, or who have a dark complexion, or who tan rather than burn, can get skin cancer. So know the risks, know what you can do to reduce them, examine your skin frequently, and be aware of any changes on it.

Death by uv Ray?

If you have ever read or seen a science fiction story, you know that the characters in such a story often go around shooting each other with ray guns. Usually, the weapons fire some form of gamma ray, which simply means that the light waves are a certain length.

Well, sci-fi authors are not all out of this world. If uv radiation, which is the stuff of all those glorious sun rays that beach bunnies love to soak up, could be concentrated into a gun, it would indeed be a killing machine. But the death of the person the gun was pointed at would be slow. The victim would perhaps notice a mole on his or her body changing border, color, or diameter. Or perhaps a blue-black dot would appear on the skin and start to slowly grow. This UV gun would give its victim skin cancer, a potentially lethal disease.

Now, consider that every time you slather on the baby oil or do not use any sunscreen, you are, in effect, pointing a UV gun at yourself. Although it is untrue to say that sunbathers are suicidal, it is quite true that they are partaking in a self-destructive activity.

If you want to live long and live beautiful, with smooth, soft skin, then use some sunscreen! (Exposure to the sun also causes premature wrinkling.) Now, I don't mean to lecture. I have spent many hours with a bikini on, letting the sun bathe me in all of its irradiating glory. I have also been to a dermatologist several times for the removal of atypical nevi from my tummy and back. The earlier you start taking care of your skin, the better. You might be able to avoid a few expensive visits to the dermatologist, some scars, and maybe a horrible illness by investing in some SPF 30.

Malignant Melanoma

Malignant melanoma is a skin cancer of the melanocytes, the population of cells that produce melanin. Malignant melanomas often have a very distinct coloring or pattern of pigment. Many are intensely black, others more blue, whereas some have brown or red patches.

How many people does malignant melanoma affect? Can it cause death? Today, the rate of increase in the number of people with melanoma is greater than for any other kind of cancer, except for lung cancer in women. Each year in the United States, the number of people diagnosed with melanoma increases approximately 7 percent. Put more simply, that means that more people than ever are getting melanoma. Although increased awareness of this disease has led to more people consulting with doctors for a skin check-up, more people are also dying from melanoma.

Although melanoma accounts for only 5 percent of all skin cancer cases, it is by far the most common cause of death of all the skin cancers. Melanoma kills. The earlier that people go to their doctors to get a funky-looking mole checked out, the less likely that the cancer has spread (metastasized). Along with its rate of occurrence, the rate of mortality (death rate) from melanoma has also been rising. Many attribute this to the increased popularity, in recent decades, of getting a tan. Now, lots of those sun babies are getting skin cancer.

There is good news about melanoma, however. The mortality rate from malignant melanoma in younger people has been holding steady in recent years, probably as a result of public education programs that emphasize prevention and early detection.

So how are these statistics relevant for you? By educating yourself and practicing proper detection and prevention techniques, you can greatly decrease the likelihood that you will ever have a malignant melanoma. If you learn how to detect an atypical nevus, you can get appropriate medical treatment before cancer has the chance to develop. Don't make the common mistake of thinking that only pale-skinned middle-aged people get melanoma. It is true that in the United States the typical person with malignant melanoma is a Caucasian female between the ages of thirty and fifty. But that does not mean, in any sense, that those are the only people who get skin cancer.

Josh

Josh is eight years old. He was brought to a dermatologist after his pediatrician noticed an abnormal-looking growth on his toe—a 4 mm. wide streak of dark tissue under his left, first toenail. After looking at it, the dermatologist was not sure what was causing this discoloration. It could have been a bruise or an infection. So the doctor took a biopsy (a tissue sample) and sent it to a laboratory for further testing.

It turned out that the growth under Josh's toenail was a malignant melanoma. Fortunately, it was very thin, and the dermatologist was able to cut it out. Josh has not had a recurrence of the cancer. The small surgical excision, or removal, cured him.

Josh was fortunate in that his lesion was found early, before the melanoma had a chance to metastasize. The lesson to be learned from Josh's story is that anyone— anyone!—can get a skin cancer, so everyone needs to be aware and stay vigilant.

Types of Malignant Melanoma

When a skin biopsy of a malignant melanoma lesion is put under a microscope, a pathologist can see several signs of cancerous change in the normal structure. Melanoma cells, which are abnormal melanocytes, can be found in the dermis and even the deeper tissues. The pathologist would also see evidence of melanocytes moving upward through the epidermis, from the basal layer toward the dead, keratinized layer.

The pathologist would also notice a phenomenon common in many types of cancer—a large number of cells in some stage of mitosis, or division. Remember that cancer cells generally divide at a much faster rate than normal cells. This is not because the cell cycle is shortened in cancer cells but because more cells are dividing than there should be in normal skin tissue. Through a microscope, the pathologist can see mitotic figures, which are the patterns that the DNA makes during cell division.

That is what a pathologist sees in a biopsy of a malignant melanoma. What does the cancer look like to the naked eye? That depends, because there are several different types of malignant melanoma. These types and their characteristics are listed below:

Lentigo Maligna Melanoma

Lentigo maligna melanoma is usually found on people older than seventy, but younger people can also get it. It is most often found on areas of skin that are exposed to the sun. These melanomas look like lentigos or big freckles that grow outward slowly while simultaneously getting a few darker spots toward the center.

The melanoma cells under these darker nodules are invading the dermis. Once these cells have broken through the basement membrane from the dermis into the epidermis, they can metastasize. Using a microscope, a pathologist would notice spindle-shaped malignant melanocytes that have replaced normal basal cells and then begun an outward, or vertical, invasion.

Superficial Spreading Melanoma

Superficial spreading melanoma accounts for the majority of melanoma in Europe, Australia, and the United States. It is found most frequently on the calves of women and on the backs of men.

This melanoma looks like an irregularly shaped, intensely pigmented area of skin. These lesions are usually fairly flat, or macular. The color can vary within one lesion, from bluish black to brown or red. Early in its development, the lesion may ooze or become crusty.

Using a microscope, a pathologist would notice melanoma cells invading upward through the epidermis and downward into the dermis.

Nodular Malignant Melanoma

Nodular malignant melanoma is most often seen in patients younger than those affected by superficial spreading or lentigo maligna melanoma. The lesion is a raised bluish-black nodule. The skin directly adjacent to and surrounding the lesion is normal.

Under a microscope, the transition between normal skin and the cancer also appears abrupt. This melanoma is characterized by deep and rapid invasion of the tissue beneath the epidermis. A pathologist needs to do a thorough examination of the specimen to make certain that the cancer cells have not invaded blood vessels or deeper tissues.

Acral Lentiginous Melanoma

Acral lentiginous melanoma usually appears on the palms of the hands and the soles of the feet. In the early stages it can look very similar to a lentigo or a benign, pigmented macular area. As it develops, a few black, nodular areas will arise.

Subungual Malignant Melanoma

Subungual malignant melanoma often masks itself as a severely stubbed toe or a fungal infection beneath the toe nail. The skin underneath the toe nail is darkly pigmented. In order to determine that this is indeed a skin cancer and not an infection or a bruise on the feet as a result of clumsiness, the dermatologist looks closely for pigment on the skin directly surrounding the nail. This is called the Hutchinson's sign. There can also be an intense inflammatory response that results in redness and swelling, since the area is easily aggravated by everyday wear and tear. This is the type of melanoma that Josh had.

Non-Melanocytic Skin Cancers

While malignant melanoma is the focus of this book, everyone should also know about the two other main types of skin cancer—basal cell and squamous cell carcinomas. Basal cell carcinoma is the most common skin cancer, and squamous cell carcinoma accounts for most of the deaths from skin cancer that do not result from malignant melanoma. The kind of skin cancer that Lynne had was basal cell carcinoma.

Basal Cell Carcinoma

Basal cell carcinoma is the most common skin tumor. Caucasians of Scottish or Irish descent are at particular risk of developing this kind of cancer. In the United States, the rate of incidence is 480 for every 100,000 males and 250 for every 100,000 females per year. Besides being of Scottish or Irish descent, risk factors include an inability to tan and large numbers of nevi on one's back. Individuals who develop basal cell carcinoma are generally elderly, although individuals with specific skin disorders (such as xeroderma pigmentosa, basal cell nevus syndrome, linear basal cell nevi) can present at a young age. Healthy people in their twenties or thirties can also develop basal cell carcinoma.

What does basal cell carcinoma look like? It generally appears as slow-growing nodules that are shiny and somewhat translucent, like a little drop of apple jelly. Over a period of one to two years, they grow to about the width of a pencil eraser. Sometimes, a small red web of tiny blood vessels is visible on the surface of the lesion.

After the nodule has grown for some time, the middle begins to ulcerate, or break open, and sinks back to normal skin level. The edges of the lesion are still raised and translucent, creating the typical "rolled, raised border" of basal cell carcinoma. Sometimes, the center will look pigmented, either because melanin is trapped with the damaged tissue or because blood vessels have broken and leaked out blood, which form little dark clots in the lesion. One type of basal cell carcinoma is even called "field fire" because the raised, red edge moves outward as the center of the lesion heals—kind of like an aerial view of a field fire.

Where does basal cell carcinoma usually show up? Ninety percent are found on the head and neck. It is found exclusively on hair-bearing skin, which has lead some researchers to believe that the basal cells of the hair follicle are somehow involved in the development of this type of skin cancer.

Basal cell carcinoma is not always found on areas of maximum sun exposure, although about one-half of basal cell carcinomas develop on the face. In regions of the world where there is more sunshine, it is more common to find basal cell carcinoma on areas of the body other than the face. A trained dermatologist will always look behind the ear of a patient at risk because this is a favorite hiding place for skin cancer.

What does a pathologist see when he looks through his microscope at a lesion from a basal cell cancer? Abnormal basal cells invading the dermis. It is as if the bricks of the first floor of our "epidermis building" are falling through the "basement" (membrane) into the ground. The basal cells that have invaded the dermis will have a large number of mitotic figures. In addition, the normal pattern of the "support beams," or stroma, of the dermis will be disrupted.

Since melanoma cells also invade the dermis, does this mean there is the same frequency of metastasis with basal cell carcinoma as with malignant melanoma? Actually, it is very rare for basal cell carcinoma to metastasize, which means that it is also very rare for it to cause death. Only 100 cases of metastasis involving this type of skin cancer have been reported, which is an extremely small percentage of all basal cell cancers. In only sixty-seven cases has the cancer even spread as far as the draining lymph node.

Basal cell carcinoma is generally treated with an excision biopsy. That is, a doctor surgically removes the entire lesion from the skin and sends it to a laboratory. There, a pathologist examines it and makes a final diagnosis.

Some people argue that this surgical cure is too aggressive. They believe that cryotherapy, or freezing the lesion, is sufficient treatment. The only problem with cryotherapy can be that it is not aggressive enough. While basal cell carcinoma can generally be treated easily, the lesions have an incredible capability for recurrence if they are not completely removed.

When the freezing method is insufficient, the cancer grows back. This rarely happens with excision biopsies. When the doctor excises the lesion, he or she cuts a little

25

healthy skin around the cancer, as a safety margin. The pathologist can then look at the specimen to make sure that no cancer cells remain in the margin. Clear margins mean that the doctor got out the entire lesion.

After the lesion has been treated, it is very important for the doctor to follow-up on the patient. With a single basal cell carcinoma, this generally means the patient receives a "skin checkup" every three to six months for a year and annually thereafter. The doctor needs to inform the patient that having had basal cell carcinoma places him or her in the high-risk group for developing all other types of skin cancer.

Squamous Cell Carcinoma

While basal cell carcinoma most commonly affects Caucasians of Scottish or Irish descent, squamous cell carcinoma is most common among white-skinned people who received a lot of exposure to the sun while they were young. The exact frequency of squamous cell carcinoma can be difficult to determine because it is often lumped together with basal cell carcinoma as "the other" skin cancer (that is, other than malignant melanoma). For this reason, most scientists believe that the usual figures given for the incidence of squamous cell carcinoma in the United States—about 136 for every 100,000 males and 59 for every 100,000 females, annually—underestimate the disease's true incidence.

Why are men more commonly afflicted with squamous cell carcinoma? The usual explanation given is that until recently, men were much more likely than women to spend significant amounts of time outdoors, especially on the job. If this is true, then the number of women and men affected by squamous cell carcinoma should become closer as more women spend time recreating and working outdoors.

Although squamous cell carcinoma is less common than basal cell carcinoma, it has a much higher mortality rate. Overall, death rates from skin cancers other than malignant melanoma are low, but squamous cell carcinoma accounts for most of those deaths.

Risk Factors

What are the risk factors for squamous cell carcinoma? In 1896, a man named Unna proposed that a lifetime of exposure to the sun was what caused "seaman's skin"— the leathery, perhaps cancer-ridden skin typical of those "old salts" who spent a lifetime working aboard ships.

Well, any person who spends a lot of time soaking in rays is equally at risk of developing seaman's skin—and squamous cell carcinoma. This includes sailors but it also applies to farmers, outdoor athletes, archeologists out on the job site, construction workers, lifeguards (like those depicted on the extremely popular television show *Baywatch*), and anyone else who spends a lot of time outside—unless they use superstrong SPF and cover as much of their skin as possible. Such people are said to have occupational exposure to the damaging UV rays of the sun. Having blond hair and blue eyes, as well as a lot of freckling in childhood, increases the risk.

In 1775, a British surgeon named Dr. Percival Pott discovered another interesting example of occupational exposure leading to skin cancer. Pott wrote a paper about a subpopulation of British men who had developed skin cancers on their scrotum—not a part of the body that commonly receives a lot of exposure to the sun. It turned out that as children these men had worked as chimney sweeps. At the time, it was common for children to work, and chimney sweeping was a common occupation for children because they were small enough to wiggle through chimneys and clean out the soot inside.

As you may have already guessed, soot is jam-packed with carcinogens (substances that cause cancers). As men, these former chimney sweeps developed squamous cell carcinomas on their scrotum because of their earlier chronic occupational exposure to carcinogens.

Although very few people still earn their living by wiggling through chimneys, squamous cell carcinoma can still occur on the genitals of men and women. The cause of these genital skin cancers is usually attributed to a sexually transmitted disease known as the human papilloma virus. This is the same virus that causes genital warts—a couple of more reasons why it is never too early to start educating yourself about the importance of safe sex, even if you are not planning to become sexually active. (If you are already sexually active, there is simply no excuse for not knowing about or not practicing safe sex.)

Another very important risk factor for squamous cell carcinoma is exposure to tobacco smoke. So add skin cancer to the list of reasons that smoking is bad for you.

Medical treatment for certain diseases can put those patients at risk for skin cancer. Psoriasis is a skin condition that can be extremely uncomfortable and cosmetically disfiguring. One of the most effective and popular treatments for severe psoriasis is called photochemotherapy.

As the name implies, this treatment involves a "photo" (light) or UV radiation component and a "chemo" (chemical) or drug component. The "photo" component involves exposing patients to a therapeutic treatment of UV exposure in a kind of light box. The "chemo" component involves treating patients with a drug called psoralen. Like UV radiation, psoralen is carcinogenic.

So why do doctors use such a treatment? In short, the benefits of photochemotherapy for people with psoriasis generally outweigh the risk of them developing squamous cell carcinoma. Even so, it is vital that their doctors inform psoriasis patients about the risk of such treatment and perform regular skin checks for the early detection of any skin cancer that does arise. Normally, about four people get basal cell carcinoma for every one person affected with squamous cell carcinoma. But among patients receiving photochemotherapy, this ratio is reversed: for every four patients who get squamous cell carcinoma, one gets basal cell carcinoma.

Other medical treatments also seem to induce skin cancer. The use of X-rays for medical diagnosis has been associated with an increased risk of skin cancer. People who have undergone an organ transplant are at a greater risk for squamous cell carcinoma. Such patients have to take large doses of immunosuppressive drugs. These medications lower the response of the body's own immune system, which would otherwise treat the new organ as an outside agent and act against it the same way it would against a disease-causing agent. Unfortunately, suppressing the patient's immune system also means reducing his or her ability to fight off disease, including skin cancer.

The fact that immunosuppression is a risk factor for skin cancer implies that the immune system plays an important anti-cancer role in the body. In any case, treatment of organ transplant patients includes follow-up for the early detection of skin cancers.

So the risk factors for squamous cell carcinoma include:

⮑ Blond hair

⮑ Blue eyes

⮑ Childhood freckling

⮑ Chronic sun exposure

⮑ Occupational or industrial carcinogen exposure

⮑ Human papilloma virus

⮑ Photochemotherapy

⮑ X-rays

⮑ Immunosuppressive drug therapy

Body Sites

So where on the body is a squamous cell carcinoma most likely to develop? They can develop on several sites on the body, but the most common place to see a squamous cell carcinoma is on the skin in areas that have been exposed to or damaged by the sun, such as the back of the hand, the forearm, the face, and the neck. Think of the classic "farmer's tan," and you will have an idea of the most common areas.

Squamous cell cancers also show up on the lower lip. Historically, this was attributed to the common practice of smoking tobacco out of clay pipes. The tar from the tobacco caused malignant changes in the cell of the skin.

These days, smoking tobacco from a pipe is not so common, but other dangerous practices have taken its place. People who smoke, dip, or chew tobacco often develop these skin cancers in their mouths. Other nonexposed areas where squamous cell carcinomas are commonly found include sites of chronic ulceration or scar tissue. An example is the skin next to bedsores of people who are forced to spend prolonged periods in bed, such as patients in hospitals or the elderly.

Squamous cell carcinomas look like small, crusty nodules that refuse to go away. Sometimes, the crusty part forms a horn cyst. These lesions actually look like little hard horns that are sticking out of the skin. Under the microscope, a pathologist will see an irregular downgrowth of epidermal keratinocytes into the dermis. Many of these invading cells will look like spindle cells. Sometimes the epidermis will no longer be attached to the dermis.

Obviously, if you find something like this on your skin, you need to see a doctor, preferably as soon as possible. If the lesion is small and the doctor suspects it might be a squamous cell cancer, then he or she will excise it entirely, with margins, and send it to the lab and a pathologist for a definitive diagnosis. If it is a larger lesion, the doctor will excise only a part of it for the lab.

How does the pathologist determine whether the tissue is a squamous cell carcinoma? These cancer cells cause a certain type of protein to be produced. The lab uses an antibody that adheres to this protein. This antibody has a label (a traceable part) that turns a certain color under the right conditions. In the lab, the labeled antibody is allowed to soak into the lesion. Then the lesion is examined under a microscope again. If the label color can be seen, then the lab knows that the protein typical of a squamous cell cancer is in the lesion, and the diagnosis is a squamous cell carcinoma. However, if the label is not visible, then the specific type of protein indicative of squamous cell carcinoma is not present.

If the diagnosis indeed is a squamous cell carcinoma, then the doctor will perform surgery to remove it. If it has already metastasized, then a form of treatment called radiotherapy may be considered. A patient with squamous cell cancer should go to follow-up visits to the doctor every three months for the first year after initial diagnosis and treatment and then every six months after that. The site of the cancer and the draining lymph nodes should be checked each time. The doctor should also advise the patient to avoid sun exposure.

Malignant Melanoma: Risk and Prevention

If you are a teenager, you probably feel that there are many aspects of your life that you do not control. You have to go to school, where your teachers tell you what they expect of you. At home, your parents may try to tell you what to eat, how you should dress, how late you can stay out, or whether you can use the car.

There is one thing you can start to take control of right now, this very minute. In fact, if you're reading this book, you already have. What is it? Your health.

You already know that smoking causes lung cancer and that substance abuse can greatly complicate your life and even kill you and others, as can unsafe sex. Now you know, if you didn't already, that hanging out in the sun without sunscreen can give you skin cancer. The question is, what are you going to do with this knowledge? Ignore it and hope for the best? Or take responsibility for your actions and control of your health and your life?

So how does this apply to melanoma? No one can prevent cancer, right? It's just something that happens to people isn't it? Well, yes and no. There is no absolute, foolproof way that can guarantee that you will never get any form of cancer, including melanoma. But there are many things you can do to greatly reduce the chance that you will get melanoma.

The first—and perhaps biggest step—toward preventing melanoma is to get your facts straight. You do this by educating yourself about the disease and its prevention. Dr. Michael Whitlow, a dermatologist from the New York University Medical Center, feels that ignorance among young people concerning malignant melanoma is an issue that demands immediate attention. "This is a real problem," Dr. Whitlow explains. "The things children and adolescents do have consequences. For melanoma, the sun exposure that people receive as children is more critical than the exposure they receive as adults."

Doctors and scientists estimate that 80 percent of the damage from the sun responsible for causing melanoma accumulates before a person reaches the age of eighteen. That means that you directly decrease your risk of getting malignant melanoma by starting to wear sunblock now. You control this risk factor.

"There are a lot of diseases that are silent killers; for years they do their damage in the absence of anyone feeling bad. It is the same thing with sun exposure," says Dr. Whitlow. The accumulation of damage from sun exposure to the DNA in your skin cells can be a "silent killer" that you nonetheless have control over. Take control and start taking care of yourself by learning about what puts you at risk for melanoma.

Sun: Shields Up

It is true that UV radiation causes non-melanocytic skin cancer in all skin types. According to many studies, however, the role of sun exposure in malignant melanoma seems to be more complicated, which is far from saying that you ought to run out to the beach and start soaking up some rays.

The mechanism by which sun exposure leads to skin cancer is still not fully understood. Using patterns that have been observed in known cases of skin cancer, researchers are trying to determine exactly how the intensity, duration, or frequency of exposure to UV radiation induces malignant change in skin cells.

With regard to malignant melanoma, some of the patterns that have been observed are a bit of a surprise. For example, malignant melanoma is more common among indoor workers than outdoor workers. It also turns out that melanoma does not predominantly occur on the body sites that are most exposed to the sun. These patterns have led researchers to conclude that melanocytes are more likely to undergo malignant change when *occasionally* rather than constantly blasted by sun radiation. This is called the intermittent sun exposure hypothesis. (A hypothesis is a theory, idea, or explanation that has not yet been conclusively proven.)

Admittedly, the intermittent sun exposure hypothesis seems somewhat illogical. If exposure to the sun is bad, doesn't it make sense that the more sun you get, the worse for you it will be? Believers in the intermittent sun exposure hypothesis explain how occasional sun exposure can be damaging. It turns out that skin regularly exposed to sunlight tries to protect itself by preventing its DNA from mutating. The number of melanocytes in the skin increases; the amount of melanin produced and taken up by keratinocytes increases; the skin's outer layer of dead skin cells becomes thicker.

So how do these things protect the skin? Melanin and dead skin cells shield the DNA of the skin cells from damaging radiation. Does this mean that regularly exposing the skin to radiation actually serves to protect the skin from malignant change? Certainly not for basal cell or squamous cell carcinoma. UV radiation from the sun, in any amount or frequency, seems to cause these cancers to develop.

Melanoma is not so simple, though. It is possible that if you tan rather than burn, a little bit of daily exposure to the sun might lower your risk of developing melanoma. But if your skin does not receive daily exposure to the sun, any rays that you do catch constitute "intermittent" exposure. These rays catch your skin cells by surprise. Unprepared for radiation, your skin has its shields down—its melanin is low and the skin is thin.

If you like, picture your skin cells as spaceships—the *Starship Enterprise* from *Star Trek* or the *Millenium Falcon* from *Star Wars*. The ship's protective shield is melanin. When enemies from another part of the galaxy come along and "shoot" UV rays at the spaceship, the melanin shield deflects the rays away. The DNA core of the spaceship is not harmed at all. However, if the spaceship is not expecting an attack and the melanin shields are down, and then a UV attack is launched . . . **BOOM!** The DNA core gets seriously damaged, in the form of mutation. Well, as far as malignant melanoma is concerned, occasional or intermittent exposure to the sun is the same as a sneak attack with the shields down.

At least according to the intermittent sun exposure

hypothesis, it is the same. However, although most cancer researchers and physicians agree that sun exposure causes non-melanocytic skin cancer (basal cell and squamous cell carcinoma), not all believe that the intermittent sun exposure hypothesis is a convincing explanation of what causes melanoma. Some researchers even believe that the sunlight hypothesis is entirely wrong and that sun exposure has little to do with the development of melanoma.

This is, admittedly, somewhat confusing, and research on the subject is nowhere near finished. But what is known for certain is still enough to guide you in responsible behavior regarding the prevention of skin cancer. And what is known for certain is this:

↪ The sun's radiation causes malignant change in skin cells that leads to both basal cell and squamous cell carcinomas.

↪ It is very likely that sun exposure plays a role in the malignant changes in skin cells that result in melanoma.

↪ Given this knowledge, it is clear that for most people, the safest thing to do is protect your skin from exposure to the sun at all times.

Dr. Ruth Oratz is an oncologist at the New York University Medical Center in New York City. An oncologist is a doctor who specializes in the study and treatment of tumors, and Dr. Oratz is a leader in the latest research regarding the use of vaccines in the treatment of cancer. Needless to say, that makes her knowledgeable about the most current theories of what causes different types of cancer. In an interview, Dr. Oratz explained what she believes to be the relationship between sun exposure and malignant melanoma like this:

"The story with sun exposure is that it is the second hit. I don't think that it is the only causative factor. Because when you go to the beach at spring break there are 20,000 people on the beach and 20,000 people are not going to get melanoma. I would say with squamous and basal cell, it is 100 percent that UV radiation is the first hit, and it's that constant sun exposure that keeps causing damage to the DNA in the skin cells—different cells though for squamous cell and basal cell.

"I think in melanoma there's something in the melanocyte that's abnormal to begin with, and the damage from the ultraviolet radiation may be the second hit. It is probably that intense burn, intermittent, as opposed to the long-term chronic sun exposure. I'm not saying that sun doesn't play a role, I'm just saying that it's not the only causative factor."

So the final lesson to be learned concerning melanoma and sun exposure is: Shields up. For those of us who do not tan, that means sunblock or shade. Right now.

Susan

Susan is the name of a young lawyer—she was twenty-six years old at the time—who made an appointment with a dermatologist because of a huge and sudden outbreak of acne on her face. While taking Susan's medical history and performing his examination, the

38

doctor noticed many moles that looked abnormal, in particular one on the back of Susan's right calf.

The doctor asked Susan if she had noticed the mole before and, if so, whether it had recently changed shape or color. Susan told the dermatologist that an acquaintance had noticed the mole at a holiday party and had suggested that she have it checked out. Because of her extremely busy work schedule, Susan put it off for months. But when the stress of her job made her face break out, she finally made an appointment with a dermatologist

The dermatologist continued to ask Susan questions about her medical history. Had she ever had a mole excised? Had she ever had skin cancer? Does she spend a lot of time in the sun?

As it turns out, Susan had been an extremely talented tennis player, good enough in high school to be rated first in her age group in the state of Florida. The state's warm climate allowed her to play and practice outside year-round. Another benefit of her dedication to the sport, as she saw it, was that she almost always sported a wicked tan—something that she misses now that she lives in the cold Northeast, works weekends, and never gets out of the office before nine at night. To compensate, she told the doctor, she always travels on her vacations to someplace warm where she can bask in the sun.

Susan's abnormal mole was a melanoma. Because it was already so thick—2.4 millimeters—the dermatologist decided that she should be referred to an oncologist. The oncologist excised a lymph node from Susan's right hip area and discovered that the *disease had metastasized. Within six months, Susan was dead.*

Fortunately, stories like Susan's are becoming much less common. This is because more people are learning how to examine themselves for the presence of any abnormal, or atypical, nevi. But Susan's story is not meant to put the blame on her—she did not know much about melanoma. Dr. Oratz emphasizes how important it is that the patient never feels as though the cancer is his or her fault: "I think that you [doctors] have to be very careful not to get into a situation where you blame the victim [the patient]. Someone gets cancer, and then it can become a kind of self-guilt thing. 'Oh, I have this terrible illness because I did something bad or I didn't do something right,' the person thinks." Instead, think of Susan's story as a real-life demonstration of the power of knowledge that leads to prevention, early detection, and early treatment.

Other Risk Factors

Besides sun exposure, what are the other risk factors that make it more likely that a person will develop a malignant melanoma? The single most important risk factor is heredity, specifically the genes a person inherits from his or her parents. Dr. Oratz explains that "people who develop melanoma, we are learning more and more, probably have some underlying predisposition to it. Particularly people who develop a malignancy at an early age most likely have some inherent susceptibility. Now that doesn't mean that someone else in your family necessarily has this illness. It means that something in the nature of your cells makes them susceptible to damage that could allow them to transform into a malignant cell."

Other important risk factors include:

⇌ Family history of melanoma in two or more first degree relatives (immediate family—mother, father, siblings, children)

⇌ Large numbers of normal melanocytic nevi (moles)

⇌ Freckles

⇌ Presence of atypical nevi

⇌ History of severe sunburn(s)

⇌ Birth and/or first few years of life spent in a tropical climate

⇌ Excessive exposure to sunlight (natural, medicinal, and/or from tanning salons)

⇌ Excessive alcohol intake (more than two drinks per day)

Under normal circumstances, moles and freckles, by themselves, are not dangerous. However, if you have a lot of moles or if you freckle at all, it can indicate that your skin is especially sensitive to UV radiation or has been exposed to a great deal of it. And skin sensitivity and high amounts of UV radiation exposure are both risk factors. Therefore, lots of freckles and moles can be a good warning sign that you need to take special care of your skin. You need to become adept at skin self-examination in addition to getting regular checkups by a dermatologist.

As the list above indicates, even one bad sunburn can be dangerous. When I was 21 years old, I had two atypical nevi excised from my stomach. My doctor told me the blistering burn I got on my stomach while sleeping for four hours at the beach in a bikini, without sunscreen, could have caused them.

"I was twelve years old then!" I said to my dermatologist. "I was twelve years old! How could my skin possibly have been affected by what happened almost ten years ago?" That was, of course, before I learned about how UV radiation damages DNA—how that damage accumulates and is passed down from cell-to-cell over many years.

With all of these risk factors, the most important thing is to be aware of your body and to be knowledgeable about your own health. In terms of melanoma, understand the genetic risk factors, which include skin type, hair and eye color, and any family history of skin disease in general and melanoma in particular.

If there is a history of melanoma in the family, you need to be even more vigilant about prevention and detection, because this history may mean that you are at a slightly increased risk for the disease. In genetic terms, the closer the relative who has had the disease is to you, the higher your risk is. A brother or sister, parent, and child are considered first-degree relatives. If a first-degree relative has had melanoma, that makes your risk somewhat greater than if a more distant relative has had the disease.

Causes

Understanding the risk factors for malignant melanoma is not the same as knowing what causes the disease. Scientists have many ideas about what causes malignant melanoma, but there is still much research that needs to be done. Educating yourself does not stop with what you learn from this book. It is important to stay aware of any new advances in research. You can ask your doctor every so often if any new risk factors for skin cancer (or other diseases, for that matter) have been determined.

Do not let your knowledge become stagnant. Refresh your knowledge about your health by keeping up with the latest developments. At the same time, be wary of the big headlines in the newspapers that proclaim a cure for cancer has been found or reveal that the cause of cancer has been discovered. If you want new information about skin cancer or another disease, ask your doctor. Even if the question does not directly concern your doctor's particular area of expertise, he or she will most likely be able to direct you toward where you can get the right answer. Knowledge is the best means of disease prevention, so keep learning.

Warning Signs

Now you know the major risk factors for melanoma and about the importance of early detection. But how, exactly, should a self-examination of the skin be done? What should you be looking for? What kind of mole is abnormal? Where should you look for atypical nevi? What are the warning signs?

Look at Yourself

Checking your skin regularly for any signs of melanoma increases the chance of finding the disease early. Because you are the person who most often sees yourself naked, you need to be the first one to spot a funny-looking mole or a new growth on your skin. The power of early detection is in your hands, but you have to train yourself to use it.

In men, melanoma is most common on the stomach, back, head, and neck. In women, melanoma is most common on the lower legs and also on the stomach and back. But remember—because melanoma can occur both in areas that are exposed to sunlight and to those that are unexposed, your self-examination needs to be complete. That means look everywhere, including behind your ears or between your toes. Your self-examination should be performed at least once a month and will take no more than five or ten minutes. That's not such a large amount of time to invest in something that will protect your health, is it?

Your Monthly Self-Exam

Designate a specific day each month, one that is easy to remember—the first day of the month, for example, or the first Friday of the month—to be the day for your monthly self-examination. A good time to do an exam is after a shower. You will need a full-length mirror, a handheld mirror, and a room with good lighting where you are ensured privacy. Then you need to:

⮯ Stand in front of a full-length mirror and check your skin for moles or other growths. Use a hand-held mirror to look at the places on your body that are hard to see, such as the back of your neck.

⮯ Perform your examination the same way every time. Start at the top and work your way down. Make sure to check your head, neck, behind the ears, under the chin, back, chest, all around each arm and leg, your hands, finger and toe nails, the bottom of your feet, between your toes, and your groin area. Your own scalp is particularly hard for you to see; after you get clothed, you can ask a friend or relative to comb through your hair and look at the skin on your scalp.

Now you know how to look at your skin. So what are you looking for? How can you tell if a mole may have become an "atypical nevus?" Because a melanoma is characterized by irregular borders and uneven or inconsistent pigment or coloring, the way to remember what kind of changes to look for is as easy as A, B, C, D. You are looking for:

⮯ **A**symmetry

⮯ an irregular **B**order

⮯ a change in **C**olor

⮯ a change in **D**iameter

If you do notice any of these changes in a mole on your skin, go to a dermatologist, immediately. The doctor is the only one who can tell you if it is an atypical nevus, pre-cancerous, or completely benign.

Dr. Oratz also warns that, "it is important to be aware that a lot of melanomas don't look like the classic ABCD melanoma. Lesions that are new, something that was never there before and now all of a sudden shows up, also warrant some attention. In addition, a regular mole shouldn't bleed, even if you shave over it. And a mole that itches should be looked at." Now you know how to use your power of detection. Pay attention to any moles that you think look weird, particularly if you think their appearance has changed. Use five to ten minutes of each month to prevent skin cancer.

Your Visit to the Doctor: A Quest

So you have decided that you need to have your skin checked out by a doctor. Many people regard going to the doctor as a terrifying experience. There is no reason why this has to be so, however. There are ways to make your doctor's appointment as comfortable and worthwhile as possible.

For many people, the worst part about a visit to the doctor is the sense that they have lost control. Like a parent or teacher, the doctor seems to be automatically in charge. This can be intimidating, especially since you are entrusting him or her with your body's well-being. It is completely normal to feel vulnerable, but there are several ways to gain a sense of control.

Before your appointment with the doctor, make a list of questions and issues you want to discuss while you are there. Dr. Whitlow, a dermatologist at the New York University Medical Center, told me that "having a list of questions is a reasonable idea, so you don't forget what you want to ask." Particularly if the office visit is going to be stressful—and it is for most people—you may forget to bring up things that you really wanted to ask. You will have enough things to think about in the doctor's office; you do not need to be worrying that you ask the right questions. So write them down before your visit.

Dr. Whitlow also mentioned several other things that a

47

patient can do to make his or her appointment more productive. Since the doctor needs to know your family's history with skin cancer and other major health issues, it will be helpful if you have informed yourself as fully as possible about these matters before your appointment. Any accurate information that you can provide helps the doctor to give you a quick and accurate diagnosis. The dermatologist will also find it helpful if you can give reasonable estimates of your sun exposure patterns, both at the present time and in the past. Dr. Whitlow also emphasizes that "if there are lesions you're particularly concerned about, be ready to point those out."

In all these ways, a patient can provide real assistance to the doctor. Doing so also helps the patient feel more in control of the situation. Even so, you may still find the appointment stressful, in particular if you are worried that what has brought you to the doctor's office might be diagnosed as cancer.

Try to keep several things in mind. Remember that a doctor spends years training in order to make sure that you get the proper diagnosis and treatment. The doctor is on your side. Think of your appointment as the beginning of a joint quest that you and your doctor are starting. The object of your quest is to discover if there is anything unhealthy going on in your body and to do everything you can to fix it.

Any experience that is unfamiliar to you will cause some amount of stress. So a good way to deal with the stress of your appointment is to learn what you can expect to happen at the doctor's office. You are in the examination room at the doctor's office, waiting. The doctor enters, the two of you introduce yourselves, and then the doctor starts to ask you some questions. A lot of questions. What the doctor is doing is called taking your history. And although it is a routine part of an examination, it is an extremely important part. Helping your doctor with your history is a very good way to help yourself.

Taking a History: What and Why

The best way to help your doctor take your history is to be prepared to answer the questions he or she asks. Here is a list of questions that you should be prepared to answer during your visit to the dermatologist for a skin cancer screening. In some cases, the reason why your doctor needs to ask these questions has also been included.

↪ Is there any history of skin cancer in your family, specifically melanoma?

↪ Has your father, mother, or sibling ever had a melanoma? You are at much greater risk of developing melanoma if a first-degree relative has or has had a melanoma. If you do not know the skin cancer history of your family, find out! If you have a first-degree relative who has had melanoma, and you have more than 100 moles and/or freckles, the likelihood that you will develop a melanoma over your lifetime is as high as 80 percent. If both of these risk factors are present, you should be checked once every six months by a dermatologist. If there is a family history of melanoma or you have more than 100 moles

49

and/or freckles, you should have a skin check by a physician once a year.

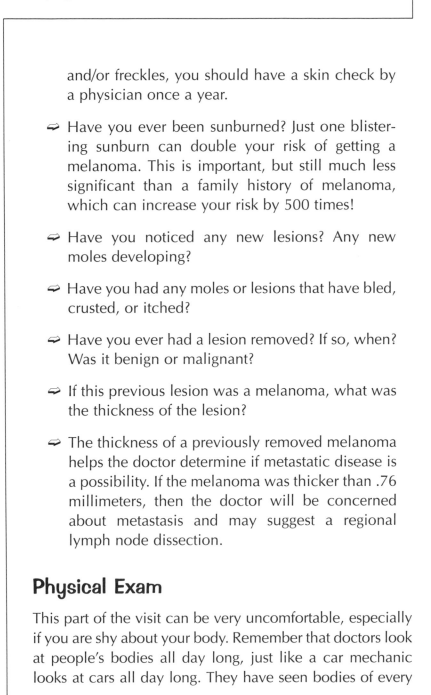

⮑ Have you ever been sunburned? Just one blistering sunburn can double your risk of getting a melanoma. This is important, but still much less significant than a family history of melanoma, which can increase your risk by 500 times!

⮑ Have you noticed any new lesions? Any new moles developing?

⮑ Have you had any moles or lesions that have bled, crusted, or itched?

⮑ Have you ever had a lesion removed? If so, when? Was it benign or malignant?

⮑ If this previous lesion was a melanoma, what was the thickness of the lesion?

⮑ The thickness of a previously removed melanoma helps the doctor determine if metastatic disease is a possibility. If the melanoma was thicker than .76 millimeters, then the doctor will be concerned about metastasis and may suggest a regional lymph node dissection.

Physical Exam

This part of the visit can be very uncomfortable, especially if you are shy about your body. Remember that doctors look at people's bodies all day long, just like a car mechanic looks at cars all day long. They have seen bodies of every shape, weight, and color. Doctors are not concerned with the variety of human form unless it constitutes a health risk. Do not worry that the doctor is going to judge your body in any way, except in evaluating its health.

Even so, you may still feel uneasy about allowing the doctor to examine your body, especially if the lesion you are concerned about is in a private area.

Dr. Oratz understands that teenage patients, in particular, can feel as if a doctor's examination is an invasion of their privacy. "A girl might be uncomfortable showing a male doctor or vice versa," she explains. "I had a young male patient who had a pigmented lesion on his penis, and he didn't want to deal with me on it. And so I sent him to someone else I knew he would be more comfortable with. But we need to be up front about what we are concerned about."

So your doctor should understand any embarrassment about how you feel. Doctors will not force you to show them anything, but you do need to tell them about what has brought you to the office. As Dr. Oratz explained, a doctor can only offer you an option that might make you more comfortable if you are upfront about your concerns. Ask your doctor to be straightforward and honest with you, and promise yourself to be the same with your doctor. Trust and honesty are essential elements of the doctor-patient relationship. You and your doctor will do better on your quest if you can trust each other along the way.

Okay, so suppose that the physical exam is going along fine, but the doctor finds a skin lesion that he or she thinks might not be entirely healthy. If the doctor does not know for sure what the lesion is, then he or she will not simply rely on the power of observation alone. The doctor then can choose one of several diagnostic procedures to try.

The doctor might take a photograph of the lesion. He or she can then measure the development of the lesion over time—particularly any change in size, shape, or color—by keeping a photographic history.

Another reason doctors take pictures of skin lesions is for education. If the lesion is unique or a perfect example of a particular type of skin disorder, a photograph can be a learning tool for other doctors or students who are training to become doctors. The photograph may be used in a classroom setting or at a medical conference, which is a meeting of doctors for the purpose of exchanging information and refining their knowledge. There is no need to worry that your name will be on the photograph or that someone who sees it will find out that it is "your" lesion. Legally, doctors cannot release any information about your medical history without your permission. As a patient, you have a right to what is called confidentiality, which means that whatever you discuss with your doctor is private will not be shared with anyone else.

The doctor's ultimate tool for diagnosis is pathological confirmation. Sending a tissue sample from the lesion to the pathology laboratory is necessary when the doctor cannot be absolutely sure of a diagnosis from observation alone. A pathology report gives a specific and very reliable diagnosis. If dermatologists use only their eyes to diagnose a lesion, they risk not treating a potentially lethal lesion or performing surgery on what was actually a totally harmless growth.

A Case History

The case history of one of Dr. Oratz's patients illustrates the importance of two aspects of the doctor visit—trusting yourself and sending a biopsy for pathological diagnosis.

> *I have another patient who was a sophomore in college. She was eighteen or nineteen and was Korean American. She had a lesion very low down on her back; it wasn't high up or in the sun at all. A mark had been there for a very long time. It had originally been diagnosed as a blue nevus, which is sometimes confused with melanoma, but it bothered her, and I think it grew or got larger. In the end it was diagnosed as melanoma.*

This case history is important for several reasons. First, it emphasizes the power of your own intuition. If you are concerned about something on your body, then you should seek a second opinion if you feel like the first doctor has brushed your concerns aside. The second point is that just like anyone else, doctors can be wrong. They will always do their best to give you a correct diagnosis, but sometimes they make mistakes. In this case, the first doctor may have thought that the likelihood of such a young woman of Korean heritage getting a melanoma was too small to consider as a possible diagnosis. The correct diagnosis was finally determined by the pathology report.

Biopsy

So a pathological diagnosis should eliminate "guesswork" from the process.

Obtaining a tissue sample for diagnostic purposes is called taking a biopsy. The dermatologist can perform two kinds of biopsy—an excisional or incisional biopsy. In an excisional biopsy, the doctor cuts out the entire lesion along with a narrow margin (usually no more than one to two millimeters) of seemingly healthy skin.

The pathologist is then able to give a specific diagnosis, which generally confirms the dermatologist's suspected diagnosis. The inclusion of the margin allows the pathologist to judge whether the entire lesion was excised. If the pathologist finds that the lesion is malignant and also discovers malignant cells in the margin, he or she will tell the dermatologist. The dermatologist will then cut out more of the surrounding area of the skin in an attempt to remove all of the malignant cells from the patient's body.

Sometimes, cutting out the entire lesion is not desirable or necessary, for several reasons. If the doctor does not think that the lesion looks harmful but wants to be certain, he or she may take an incisional biopsy. In an incisional biopsy, only a part of the lesion is cut out and sent for pathological analysis. Other reasons for performing an incisional rather than an excisional biopsy might be that the lesion is very large or on a person's face. In either of these cases, the patient may prefer knowing for sure that the lesion is malignant before undergoing surgery.

In either case, the biopsy procedure does not make the lesion any more harmful. Studies have shown that neither biopsy procedure worsens the patient's prognosis or odds of recovery.

In a excisional biopsy, the doctor uses a scalpel to cut out the lesion. For a incisional biopsy, the doctor uses a scalpel or performs a punch biopsy procedure. In a punch biopsy, the doctor uses a device somewhat like a hole puncher you might use on papers, except in this case it punches out a small part of your skin. The tissue specimen then gets put in a little jar in fluid that helps maintain the cells in their natural state.

At the Pathology Lab

So your office visit is over, and now you go home and wait for someone at the doctor's office to call and tell you the results from the pathologist's laboratory. While you are waiting, what is the pathologist doing to figure out exactly what is going on in that lesion?

A trained pathologist can probably see skin layers and cells in his or her sleep. One of the most basic skills of the pathologist is simply looking at a specimen under the microscope. By coloring the cells of the specimen with specific dyes that stain structures certain colors, the pathologist can see the changes that indicate if the lesion is squamous cell carcinoma, basal cell carcinoma, or malignant melanoma—or better yet, that it is not cancerous at all.

There are many different types of stains that can be used, and the pathologist is familiar with them all. Although a trained pathologist can tell a lot just from looking at tissue through a basic light microscope, this approach still has limitations. One of these is the fact that this kind of microscope only can magnify an object so much. Although the pathologist learns much just by looking at the general arrangement of the cells and their basic positions in relationship to each other, there are more specific and exact methods of diagnosing a skin lesion.

The pathologist may look at one cell in extreme detail under an electron microscope. This allows the structures within a potentially malignant cell to be studied in detail. A pathologist might do this if he or she is not quite sure from what kind of cell the tumor originated.

A new, common, and extremely reliable diagnostic technique that pathologists use is called immunocytochemistry. The pathologist takes a tissue specimen and soaks it in a solution that has a large amount of a specific protein in it. The pathologist knows a lot about the structure of this protein. Proteins, like any molecule, like to stick to other molecules. The pathologist knows specifically what molecule(s) this protein likes to hang around.

The protein in the solution is given a chance to latch on to its "friend" molecules. Then the pathologist washes the tissue off and lets it soak in another solution. This second solution has a special dye in it that sticks to the protein in the first solution. The dye allows the pathologist to see if and where any protein stuck to the tissue that is being tested. This allows him or her to define, with nearly absolute precision and little risk of human error, what kind of cell is in the lesion.

The most precise diagnostic technique is DNA analysis. The pathologist obtains DNA from the cells in the lesion and studies the composition at specific places that are known to dictate cell type and/or malignant potential. Generally, doctors do not use DNA analysis to diagnose lesions from a normal doctor's visit. It is a very expensive procedure and is most often used in a research setting, where it is allowing scientists to understand the process more fully of how cancer develops at the level of the chromosomes.

Do I Have Malignant Melanoma?

Waiting to learn the results of the lab report can be very frustrating and scary. Try to put it out of your mind as much as possible. If you or the doctor think that cancer is a real possibility, try to plan some activities with your friends or your family that will keep you busy until you get your results back. The lab usually takes a couple of weekdays to send a report back to your doctor. Some doctors will call you when they have your results; others will ask you to call the office a day or so after your appointment.

If you know when you are likely to find out your results, try to arrange to have someone with you for support. Your parents may want to hear the news first so that they can explain it to you if the news is not so good. Keep an open ear. Your parents may be very scared for you. Talk with them and discuss who is going to talk to the doctor. If you have two phones in the house, you may decide to get on the phone together with the doctor. In any case, while you are waiting, try not to imagine the worst possible outcome. Think positively. It can be hard to do, but it really helps.

And if you do indeed have a malignant melanoma? Remember that skin cancer can be treated successfully when found early enough. And there are a lot of things that you can do to help that treatment succeed.

Learning That You Have Cancer

"You have cancer." These three words can be the most terrifying you will ever hear. When you first learn that you have malignant melanoma, you may be overwhelmed by emotions. It is important that you know that any emotion you feel is normal. Be honest with yourself. If you feel angry, do not push it away. If you feel like crying, go ahead and cry. Trying to regulate or judge your emotions only adds to your stress, and that is the last thing that you need.

Denial

While Melissa was sitting in the doctor's office, holding her mother's hand, she really didn't think that she would be diagnosed as having cancer. It couldn't be possible, could it? For one thing, she had too much she needed to do. She needed to get this appointment over with and get back to school for the literary magazine meeting.

Her mom was freaking out. The whole way over to the doctor's office, on the bus, Melissa had to calm her down. Now, in the office, she had to hold her hand. "Come on, Mom," Melissa was thinking. "Get a hold of yourself! I'm seventeen. I don't have skin cancer."

Then the doctor came in. "Melissa, I am sorry to tell you that you have cancer, a cancer of the skin called malignant melanoma," said the doctor.

"Oh, dear God!" said Melissa's mom.

Melissa sat in the chair, concentrating on the doctor's desk. There was no way the doctor was right.

"Melissa? Do you understand what cancer is?" asked the doctor, who had come from behind her desk and stepped into Melissa's view.

"Yeah, I know what it is," Melissa replied, "but I can't have skin cancer. Are you sure the tests were correct?"

Melissa had entered the doctor's office denying the possibility that she had skin cancer. Her mother has always done the worrying for everyone in the family, so Melissa was not used to taking a situation seriously until she directly felt its effect. Now, the doctor has told her she has cancer, but Melissa cannot digest this information yet. She cannot accept the whole truth of her situation. A psychiatrist, psychologist, or therapist would say that she is in denial about the fact that she has cancer. Denial is a very common emotional response to a stressful situation, especially one in which you feel your own ability to respond or exercise control is extremely limited.

Confusion

Another common response to the words "you have cancer" is confusion. Do not be ashamed or embarrassed if there are things about having cancer or malignant melanoma that you do not understand. Ask your doctor anything you want to know. Any question you have about your body and cancer is very important. Your parents may have a lot of questions, too. Listen closely to what they ask, and try to learn from the doctor's replies. Your parents' questions may not be the same ones that you would ask, but they are important nonetheless. Maybe they will even think of some that you would not have.

Shock

You may need to undergo extensive surgery or treatment as soon as possible. The doctor may even want you to go in to the hospital for treatment that very day. What about school? The date you have with Josh? The play you are rehearsing for? The track meet on Friday? Unfortunately, cancer and its treatment can turn your world upside down in no time at all. Not only have you been told that you have cancer, but now you are being asked to change your daily routines without any time to process the whole situation.

Anger

Anger is a very common—and quite normal—response to learning that you have cancer. You may get very angry in general—at doctors, at the hospital staff, even at friends and family. That's okay. You are probably angry at the injustice that this all had to happen to you. Try to vent your anger in a non-destructive way. If you find yourself becoming upset with someone about something specific, ask them to let you cool off before you explain the problem to them. The people closest to you should understand your anger, but try to channel all of that energy into fighting the cancer, not yourself and all of those around you.

Solitude

You may feel like you just want to be left alone. No one else seems to understand exactly what you are going through, and you certainly do not want their pity. It seems so much easier to lie in your room and watch television or read or put on your headphones to listen to music for hours.

If you do feel the need to be alone, try to make that time alone productive. That does not necessarily mean that you should be doing homework or cleaning out your closet, but try to be productive for yourself and your well-being. You feel the need to isolate yourself because you are overwhelmed by the situation and your emotions and, perhaps, cannot deal with everyone else's reactions on top of it all.

So when you feel the need to yell, "Just leave me alone!" and to lock yourself in your room, use your time to process what is going on. Ask yourself why you are angry or sad or why you cannot take anymore so-and-so or why you just do not care, if that is what you are feeling. If you need to tune out by listening to music or gazing at the television, fine, but allowing your emotions to fester and simmer can be bad for you.

A positive attitude can assist your ability to fight off

disease, especially cancer. This is not self-help mumbo-jumbo, but medical fact. So instead of closing the door on the world and your emotions, try to process what you are feeling. The sooner you accept and understand your emotions, the sooner you can develop an attitude about your cancer that will encourage, not discourage, your recovery.

One idea that has worked for other people in the same situation is keeping a journal. You do not need to know exactly what you want to write about. Just sit down and write about whatever is on your mind at that point, or what happened that day and how it made you feel. Do not censor yourself; your journal is just for you. Do not concern yourself with what other people would think if they could read what you have written. This is for you, not for them. You will find that your mind has a funny way of figuring out what you need to think about and process.

Loneliness

It's a funny thing. Sometimes you feel like slamming the door in everyone's faces, while at other times you feel like no matter what you do you are always alone. You can feel absolutely isolated even when you are surrounded by people who may be actively trying to include you in activities or in conversation.

These are totally normal reactions to a situation as emotionally difficult as coping with melanoma. When you feel lonely, ask for company. Be honest with those around you. If you want some time alone, ask for that, too.

Stress

Stress is a very powerful force. It has been shown that stress and anxiety can actually reduce the strength of your immune system. In order to muster the strength that you need to get healthy, you need to know what you can do to reduce the stress of your situation.

One thing you can do is remember what strong resources you have to draw on—specifically, what is inside you. In this case, don't draw so much on your tissue and organs and blood vessels, but on all the character traits that make you the remarkable individual you are. The great nineteenth-century American poet and philosopher Ralph Waldo Emerson put it like this: "What lies behind us and what lies before us are small matter compared to what lies within us."

One of the major sources of stress for you may be worries about your future . . . will you get to go to college? Get married? Visit the Grand Canyon? Go bungee jumping? Or do whatever it is you have dreamed about doing since you can remember? Worrying about the future and the "what ifs" of your situation can be very stressful and depressing. Try to reserve your energy for the challenge at hand—getting better. No one, with or without cancer, can possibly know if they will fulfill all their dreams. Constantly worrying about the future, whether you are healthy or not, is counterproductive. Spending energy on thinking about the future will only mean that you have less energy to spend on the present. And it is by acting now that you create your future. Spend your energy on the present.

Treatment Options

One of the most discouraging things about learning you have cancer is the feeling it creates of having no choice about what is going to happen to you next. But you have many choices, and many decisions to make. One of the first—and most important—concerns your treatment. The doctor can recommend a specific course of treatment and provide you with other options, but the choice has to be yours.

Surgery

The most totally reliable treatment for malignant melanoma is complete surgical excision. If your biopsy required a complete excision, that may be the only treatment you need. If the lesion was small and the pathologist found clear margins around the biopsy, then you may not need any further treatment.

In such a case, the hope is that all of the malignant cells have been removed. Make sure that you take care of the wound exactly as your doctor directs. The most important thing is to avoid infection. Your skin, remember, is your body's natural barrier between your insides and the outside world. It does the best it can to keep bacteria and other microscopic organisms from getting into your body and producing infection.

When your skin is cut, whether it happens during a soccer game or during surgery, this natural barrier is broken, and bacteria can make your body their playground. If your doctor recommends a topical antibiotic, such as Neosporin, make sure that you know how to use it properly. Ask your doctor to describe the warning signs of infection to you. That way, you can get help before an infection becomes a major problem.

An excisional biopsy should not leave much of a scar. Although there is no medical evidence to prove it, popular wisdom has it that cocoa butter lotion helps reduce scarring. I tried it when I was recovering from knee surgery, and it worked for me.

If the surgery needs to be more extensive than the initial excisional biopsy, the wound may be larger and scarring is more likely. Not too many people like the idea of having a permanent scar, particularly on their face. For males, the prospect of a scar may not be as difficult to handle as it is for females. Many women, including myself, think that a scar on a man's face can be kind of sexy. Many male film and television stars, including Harrison Ford and Jason Priestley, have facial scars. Other men often think that scars on a man are kind of cool, a badge of toughness or ruggedness.

Unfortunately, the same attitudes seldom apply to women. Scars on women are not usually regarded as sexy or cool. Even so, the attitude you take about any of your imperfections, including a scar, will dictate the attitude other people take, more often than not. Look at some of the women who are celebrated in the media, such as the Spice Girls, Janet Jackson, or Madonna. Each of them do their own thing and do it with pride. People are attracted to that positive energy. Madonna has a big space between her teeth and no one cares, right? Constantly worrying about an imperfection only draws attention to it. If you act as if the scar is no big deal, then most people you deal with will probably respond the same way. If they don't, let that be their problem, not yours.

Even once you no longer need a bandage on the area, your skin is still healing. While it is healing, this new skin is very sensitive to sunlight, so you should put a high SPF lotion on that area anytime that you are going to be outside. This new skin is very sensitive to sunlight. Protecting it from ultraviolet radiation will ensure that no discoloration of the skin occurs.

Ask your doctor for advice about how to reduce scarring. Plastic surgery can have great cosmetic results. Your dermatologist may have a plastic surgeon with whom he or she works closely. Ask about this possibility.

Cryotherapy

Cryotherapy is another treatment option for malignant melanoma. In cryotherapy, the doctor uses a small stream of frozen nitrogen gas to freeze the lesion. The freezing kills the malignant cells.

Metastasis

Surgery and cryotherapy have proven to be successful treatments for malignant melanoma. But if the disease has already metastasized, or spread, deep into the dermis or into other structures or organs, other methods of treatment become necessary. You may have to undergo even more extensive surgery that involves removing malignant tissue from an important organ, such as the lung or liver. A surgeon cannot always remove all of the cancer cells, however. In such cases, other kinds of treatment that kill cancer cells must be found.

Chemotherapy

Some cancers can be treated with drugs. This is called chemotherapy, or chemo for short. The drugs stop the cancer from spreading by inhibiting the malignant cells from multiplying. Unfortunately, the drugs cannot tell the difference between malignant cells and normal cells. The drugs simply do not allow cells, of any type, to multiply. This means that the places in your body that contain cells that constantly or rapidly multiply are going to be affected by chemotherapy, even if they are healthy.

This is why some people lose their hair while undergoing chemotherapy. Hair loss, in fact, might be the best known side effect of chemotherapy. Hair follicles are sites where cells are constantly proliferating to make new hair. Chemotherapy interferes with this process, with the result that a patient often loses some or all of his or her hair. The good news is that such hair loss is almost always reversible, meaning that the hair grows back once chemotherapy is stopped. Sometimes the hair even grows back a different color or texture.

In terms of your physical health, hair loss is not considered a particularly major side effect. But there is no denying that it can be emotionally devastating. Again, guys may have an easier time dealing with this, although few men, especially young men in their teens, are ever happy about losing their hair. Even so, a man can shave his head, and it becomes a kind of fashion statement. Just look at Michael Jordan and dozens of other stars of the National Basketball Association. Or a man can wear a baseball cap, which is a hip fashion accessory just about everywhere, anyway.

It is true that society tends to be less accepting of bald women. Even so, women who experience hair loss from chemotherapy have several options. If you have the guts, shave it all off! Some women do, and it gives them a courageous, exotic air that can be very attractive. You can cover your head with hats or scarves and use them to create a unique sense of personal style. Scarves and bandannas come in virtually every color of the rainbow and in almost every imaginable fabric. If you use a bigger scarf, one made of cotton or silk or a thin fabric of some sort, you can tie it around your head and let the leftover part hang down your back. That way, if you have a habit of twirling your hair or playing with it, you can use the tail of your scarf for the same purpose. Who knows, it is even possible that you will find that you do not miss having to fuss with your hair every morning.

The other option is wearing a wig. Wigs can be expensive, but they are a tax-deductible medical expense and some insurance plans cover the price. Find out whether your insurance will cover the cost before you spend a lot of money. The best idea is a wig made of synthetic fibers rather than real hair. The synthetic fibers are easier to wash and dry and keep your head cooler while you are wearing the wig. The real ones can make your scalp pretty sweaty.

The other place in your body where cells are multiplying in large number is in the bone marrow. The bone marrow is where blood cells are produced. For this reason, chemotherapy can seriously affect your bone marrow. The result, most often, is a reduction in the amount of certain kinds of blood cells.

If your red blood cell count becomes lowered, the ability of your blood to carry oxygen to your tissues is lowered. Since oxygen is the fuel for your cells, the result can be a loss of energy. So you should not be surprised if you feel more tired than usual once you start chemotherapy. If this happens, don't feel that you have to keep up with your earlier schedule. The most important thing in your life now is getting well. Let yourself sleep when you need to. Take naps during the day. Your body is under stress and has less fuel than usual to work with, so give yourself a break. Try to take it easy, and do not feel guilty for not being as productive or energetic as you normally would be.

If your white blood cell count becomes lowered, your body's immune system works less efficiently. White blood cells are the mainstay of your immune system. When the number of a person's white blood cells is reduced, doctors say that the person is immunosuppressed. That is why if you do receive chemotherapy, your doctor will monitor your white blood cell count. The lower it gets, the easier it becomes for bacteria or viruses to infect your body.

Even perfectly healthy people get infections, of course, but they are particularly dangerous for people who are immunosuppressed, because their immune system is not at full strength to fight off infection. The doctors and staff at the clinic or hospital where you receive your chemotherapy will take special precautions to make certain that they do not infect you while you are being treated. You should ask them what you can do to avoid infection while you are going about the rest of your day-to-day life. They may tell you that the best way is simply to stay positive, eat well, and reserve your energy.

Each of those things is easier said than done. For example, eating well does not sound as if it should be too difficult, but chemotherapy can decrease your appetite. It is extremely important that your body is fed well while you are going through this difficult time, no matter what kind of treatment you need. A nutritious diet can make a huge difference in your body's ability to undergo treatment and fight off cancer successfully. It allows you to endure the side effects of treatment better and therefore to undergo higher doses of chemotherapy or other treatments. As you know, both cancer and treatment can damage healthy cells. By eating well, you give your body the building blocks it needs to repair and build cells.

In addition to feeding your body, you need to feed your mind. Eating well can improve not only your physical well-being but also your mental well-being. You know how cranky and tired you can get when you are absolutely starving for dinner? Well, your body needs you to have a positive attitude and enough energy to stay strong mentally.

However, with chemotherapy, you may have a difficult time eating at all, let alone eating a balanced meal.

Your doctors or a nutritionist at the hospital should be able to tell you what types of food you need the most. You definitely need lots of protein because it is one of the main building blocks for cells. Dairy products (including ice cream, cheese, and pudding), beans, and peanut butter are all very high in protein. You can have as many milk shakes a day as you want! Now is not the time to worry about gaining weight. Unless your doctor tells you that you need to cut down on the calories, eat all you can. Your body needs all the energy it can get.

But how can you maintain a healthy diet when the chemo makes you nauseous? Well, when you feel as though you can eat, try to eat food high in calories, protein, and vitamins. Spread some peanut butter on toast and put some banana slices on top, or make a shake with fruit and ice cream. If you feel sick, do not force yourself to eat, but even if you feel really sick, make sure you keep drinking fluids.

On those not-so-great days, try to drink milk or juice if you can. When you feel like you can keep food down, try to get your appetite going. Sometimes it helps to create a restaurant atmosphere where you are eating. Put on some music, if you can, and lower the lights a bit. Ask a friend or relative to come eat with you. Relax and eat as much as you can. Eat your favorite foods at all times if you can. If you get weird cravings, allow yourself to eat anything you want, at any time of day. If you are hospitalized while undergoing treatment, the hospital staff will bring you food at all hours—even at four in the morning—because they know how important it is that you take advantage of the times you are hungry.

Radiation Therapy

Malignant cancer cells are often treated using radiotherapy. Radiation, as it is commonly called, basically kills cells by irradiating them with high-energy rays of light. Radiotherapy can cause headaches and loss of energy. Like chemotherapy, radiation does not distinguish between normal cells and malignant cells. Doctors use several methods to guide the rays, but sometimes the tissue surrounding the radiation target area still gets damaged.

If you need radiation therapy to the head or neck, you may experience hair loss. Unfortunately, hair loss from radiation, unlike that from chemotherapy, can be permanent. Your hair may fall out in patches and may not grow back. Coping with permanent hair loss can be difficult. Your options are generally the same as with the temporary hair loss caused by chemotherapy. Most likely, however, you probably will not have to deal with this issue. Generally, radiotherapy is not a treatment option for malignant melanoma, which has proven to be pretty much "radio-resistant."

New Developments in Treatment

Overall, malignant melanoma does not respond as well as other cancers to chemotherapy either. Malignant melanoma has proven to be a very difficult cancer to treat.

Currently, many experimental treatments for melanoma are being researched and tested. At most major hospitals, you can apply to be a part of a research program or clinical trial, although it can be difficult to get accepted. The

doctors running the program will have certain require-
ments for the kind of patients they want to be involved.
These might include a range of ages, an exact type and/or
stage of skin cancer, and other even more specific factors.
Remember that these experimental treatment options are
not necessarily going to be better than existing options
simply because they are new and on the "cutting edge" of
cancer research. If they had been conclusively proven to
be effective and without harmful side effects, they would
no longer be considered experimental.

Biological Therapy

The most recent advance in the treatment of skin cancer
actually has nothing to do with cutting or surgery. Many
scientists now believe that cancer develops, in part, when
the immune system does not work like it should. It may be
that cancer cells exist in places in the body frequently but
that healthy immune systems are able to recognize these
abnormal cells and kill them off.

When cancer cells are not killed, they can multiply and
become a clinically manifested disease. This happens
when the immune system does not recognize and kill the
cancer cells.

So scientists suggest that it might be a good idea to treat
cancer by bolstering the immune system. It is kind of like
when you need a lot of energy to play at your maximum
ability in a soccer match against the rival school. Your
body would be wasting time if it had to go to its energy
reserves, like fat, and break them down into sugar and
then ship the sugar out into the circulatory system. You do

not have that time, because the clock on the scoreboard has already started. So instead you eat one of those chewy high-energy bars. Now all of those molecules of sugar race around your body to serve the needs of your muscles and brain so you can kick the heck out of the other team.

Biological therapy works in a similar fashion. Your immune system needs many different kinds of signaling molecules to do its job, but now that you have cancer, the fastest way to get these would be if you could just "eat" a bunch. Well, getting an injection into your blood system might be even faster. In biological therapy, doctors give a patient a boost of molecules that naturally play a part in the immune system. These molecules race around the body to serve the needs of the immune system, allowing the patient to fight off the cancer.

This approach toward treatment is a beautiful and elegant concept. Researchers attempt to guide the body's natural powers in order to fight the cancer process. Some attempts at biological therapy have been more successful than others, but such treatment holds great promise.

Historically, a group of molecules called interferons have been of interest in the treatment of cancer. There have been many clinical trials, which are a specific kind of experimental treatment program, involving interferon. Currently, interferon is administered to patients after they have had surgery in the hope that it will reduce the risk that any cancer cells left in the body will metastasize.

This kind of prevention therapy is called postoperative adjuvant therapy. Scientists disagree about its effectiveness, however. Some researchers believe that interferon has allowed patients to stay disease-free for years past the average. Others say that there does not seem to be any change in survival rate.

These two statements do not necessarily contradict each other. When doctors and scientists discuss the success of a treatment, they mean how well that treatment extends and improves quality of life. The survival rate, by contrast, means how much the treatment actually changes the likelihood that the cancer will end in death. So a treatment can be successful without changing the survival rate. That is, it might increase the lifetime of a person with cancer, and improve the quality of that person's life with cancer, without reducing the likelihood that the person eventually will die of cancer. This seems to be the case with interferon. Interferon may extend the life of a person with malignant melanoma by an average of one year, but it does not seem to affect the rate of survival.

Whether interferon improves the quality of the life it may be extending is also debatable. One aspect of most kinds of cancer treatment, including chemotherapy and radiation, is toxicity. As we have discussed, many cancer therapies have the potential to cause uncomfortable, even painful side effects. Interferon is no exception. Interferon is actually the molecule that the body naturally produces in high amounts in response to the flu. You know those achy, sleepy, feverish symptoms of the flu? Well, that is actually the side effect of the interferon, not the actual flu virus. Although it makes you feel terrible, if your body did not produce interferon in response to the flu, the result—complete infection by the flu virus—would be even more horrible, possibly even fatal. So patients undergoing interferon therapy can feel as if they have a severe case of the flu, with all the usual symptoms—aches and pains, headache, nausea, fever, extreme fatigue. If you are considering interferon therapy, it is a good idea to plan to cut down on your normal activities, as there may be a lot of time when you feel tired and generally less than 100 percent. Keep your intake of fluids high and try to eat as much as you can when you feel up to it. You can also take the normal painkillers that you would take to treat the flu. Ask your doctor which one will work the best. He or she may even prescribe something to help you deal with the side effects.

Try to remember that every person reacts differently to treatment. Do not expect to feel horrible, because that expectation can cause stress that can, by itself, make you feel pretty nauseous. Be prepared for the possible side effects, but try to build a wall of emotional strength and positivity before they have a chance to make you feel rotten. A positive attitude can actually lessen the physical discomfort.

Other molecules such as retinoids, which are similar to vitamin A, and cytokines, the immune system's main messengers, have been given to cancer patients in an attempt to boost the immune system. Some of these treatments have turned out to be too toxic; others have not been shown yet to extend life or the survival rate.

Many researchers at the most respected schools and institutes continue to try to pinpoint the best molecule to use for biological therapy. Some have discovered that maybe there is a better way to get these molecules into the circulation of the patient.

Some researchers believe that because most of these

signaling molecules are proteins that are created when the cell's machinery reads the script written on the DNA of the cell's genome, gene therapy may prove to be the best way to get more immune system molecules into the patient's body. Gene therapy involves getting some of the patient's DNA and changing it. In this case, scientists add or insert a piece of DNA script that tells the cell to make more of a certain molecule, such as a cytokine. That cell and all of its daughter cells will now be factories for that cytokine, producing mass amounts. So instead of having a protein injected, the patient can now make more of the molecule necessary to fight the cancer. Although gene therapy is a promising idea, scientists do not know yet how successful it will be for the treatment of malignant melanoma.

Another way scientists are trying to guide or bolster the immune system is by letting it know who the enemy is. When you receive a vaccination from your pediatrician or internist, the vaccine contains little bits of the enemy's coat or shield. These bits may be part of the virus's coat or the bacteria's outer wall. Your immune system sees these little signals of the enemy and builds up its supply of weapons against that particular enemy. Now when your body is invaded by a virus, a bacteria, or an abnormal cell, your immune system recognizes it immediately and employs its various molecular weapons. Because it has been so well prepared by vaccination, your immune system has no problem killing off the enemy before it has damaged your body.

Some researchers are exploring vaccination as a treatment option against malignant melanoma. The tumor vaccine would contain pieces of the cellular machinery that exists only in melanocytes. In theory, the vaccine promotes an immune response against these transformed melanocytes. Your body will produce more weapons against these cells than it was able to without the vaccine. Wherever the malignant melanocytes have metastasized will become a battlefield between your immune system and your own melanocytes.

Dr. Oratz is a leader in melanoma vaccine research. She and her colleagues run clinical trials of the melanoma vaccine. She has seen definite improvements in the immune response of patients to the cancer after administration of the vaccine. Some patients, in particular, like the one described below, have enjoyed extremely positive results.

Clara

Clara was diagnosed with melanoma when she was seventeen. She had a primary lesion on her chest and underwent sentinel node biopsies to lymph node groups in both axillas, or underarms. A very good swimmer and an extremely smart young woman, Clara chose not to go on interferon because of the side effects.

Although Clara was too young to be included in the clinical trial of the melanoma vaccine—the minimum age for the trial was eighteen—an exception was made for her. Clara was given the vaccine. The injection process requires many visits to the medical center where it is administered, but it has virtually no side effects. The only thing Clara noticed was a slight swelling and itching at the site of injection, but that only lasted for a few days.

Clara went off to college a year after she had been diagnosed. She has been doing well and functioning normally ever since.

Clara's story is one reason why researchers are so excited about the melanoma vaccine. The program that Clara took part in is located at the Kaplan Cancer Center at New York University Medical Center, but clinical trials for melanoma vaccines are being conducted all over the country. If you are interested in participating or even in learning more about them, your oncologist should be able to supply you with the appropriate information and referrals.

Clinical Trials

So with no guarantee that a new or experimental treatment will work better than other methods, how do you decide whether to take part in a clinical trial?

First you need to know exactly what a clinical trial is. Treatments are tested first on laboratory animals. After a new treatment has proven to be safe and effective when used on laboratory animals, researchers need to learn how it will work on humans. Before a new method can be offered to the public as a treatment option, it must be tested numerous times under specific guidelines established by the Food and Drug Administration (FDA), which is an agency of the federal government. This is the clinical trial stage. A treatment has to pass the clinical trial stage before it can be offered by physicians as a proven treatment for cancer.

Clinical trials must determine more than if a new treatment actually works. A clinical trial consists of three separate phases. Each phase of the trial is used to determine specific things about the treatment.

Phase I

Phase I trials are concerned with the safety or toxicity of the new treatment. Patients who volunteer for Phase I trials put themselves at great risk for experiencing painful or uncomfortable side effects, with no guarantee that the treatment will even prove to be effective for their cancer.

Most patients who enter Phase I trials are individuals who have no other options. They have tried all the traditional treatments, and nothing has worked. Usually, their cancer is at an advanced stage. People who volunteer for Phase I trials are truly giving of themselves for the advancement of cancer research.

Phase II

Phase II trials are aimed at learning about the effectiveness of the treatment. Phase II trials determine what kind of cancers respond best to the new treatment and how well it works. Usually the patients who volunteer for this phase have a cancer that has proven hard to fight with existing treatment programs.

Phase III

Phase III trials compare the new treatment with existing treatments. Patients who volunteer for Phase III trials are split into two groups. One group is treated with a traditional method, and the other receives the new treatment. The patients themselves are not told if they are in the first or the second group.

Phase III trials generally ensure that the patients involved receive the best treatment available, either from an existing method or the new one. If a treatment reaches Phase III, it means that it has already proven to be relatively safe and effective. Many patients want to take part in these trials because they want to receive the best treatment available. Phase III trials involve hundreds of patients across the country at many different hospitals and clinics.

So how do you decide whether to participate in a clinical trial? It is important to understand where on the spectrum from Phase I to Phase III you are. Do you have other options? Do you have an unusually difficult cancer to treat? Ask yourself what you hope to gain by participating. Do you want fewer side effects? Do you want to achieve remission?

The final step in your decision-making process is to learn as much as possible about the new treatment, especially regarding the answers to the previous questions. Can you hope for cure or remission? Can you hope for a break from painful side effects? Make sure that the doctor who explains the trial to you uses words you understand. Ask as many questions as you can and be sure that the doctor gives clear and specific responses.

If you decide to enter a clinical trial, you will be asked to sign an informed consent form. Basically, this is a contract that says that you have been informed of the details of the treatment and of all the possible side effects. Do not sign unless you have in fact been informed about all of these details in ways that you can understand.

Make sure that a parent or guardian also examines this form. It is always good to have someone you trust go over these things with you. Sometimes your emotions, in particular the hope that a new treatment might help, can make it difficult for you to see the possible disadvantages of entering a trial. Remember that clinical trials are never specifically focused on you as an individual. The primary goal of a clinical trial is to increase what science knows about cancer and its treatment.

In the Hospital

All of the treatment options that we have discussed are given on either an inpatient or an outpatient basis. If you are an outpatient, that means you schedule individual appointments at a clinic or hospital to receive your treatment appointment and then leave when the treatment is done. You then return again for your next appointment, until you have completed the entire recommended course of treatment.

If you are an inpatient, that means that you need to stay in the hospital for some period of time while receiving treatment. The amount of time can vary, as can the reasons why you need to be treated on an inpatient basis. The doctors may be concerned about the possibility of infection, so they want to keep you in the hospital, where you can be treated immediately if you develop a high fever or another symptom of infection. The doctors also may want to keep you in the hospital until you enter remission, which can take months.

So how can you make the best of a hospital stay? First,

remember why you are there. You are in the hospital to live. You have a job to do. You are not there to waste your time while the doctors and nurses poke and prod you. You are there to fight your cancer. With its white walls and ugly view—that is, if your room even has a window—the hospital may seem like a prison sometimes. Try instead to think of it as a safe environment where the nurses and doctors come every day to help you kill off that cancer.

Whether you have a whole room to yourself or share a room with some other patients, making the space your own can really help. If you are going to be there for some time, cover those ugly walls with posters from home. Ask your parents or brothers and sisters to bring in photos of home, your friends, vacations, and other memorable places and times. Put them up on the walls or hang them on the curtain that goes around your bed, if the nurses will let you. That way when the doctors come and pull the curtain closed, you will not feel so alone; you will be surrounded by your family and friends.

Bring in a Discman or Walkman so you can listen to music or the radio, as loud as you want to. If you have a favorite teddy bear or blanket, do not be ashamed to have it with you. Even adults cuddle with stuffed animals while they are hospitalized. Anything that makes you feel less lonely and more at home is fine. Not only is it fine, it is helpful. Anything that helps you feel better aids you in fighting cancer.

Do not worry about what friends or family or the doctors will think. They want you to be happy and strong. If having your favorite stuffed bear, Pancake, with you makes you happier, then keep him there with you. You will probably receive a lot of cards and flowers from people you know. If all the flowers get to be too much, keep your favorite ones or the ones from your favorite people. Ask the nurses or your parents to give the other flowers to people who do not have as many. Or perhaps they can put them in the common waiting rooms or recreation rooms. You can make a big display of the cards you get on your curtain or wall. Or you may just want to collect a pile on your bedside table.

You will probably receive visitors, especially from your family. You may find yourself feeling like you have to make conversation with people whom you normally do not talk to all that much. On top of that, they may feel uncomfortable because they do not know what to say to you or how to make you feel better. Or at times you simply might feel tired or not up to talking.

Do not feel that it is your responsibility to entertain visitors. Try to express thanks; tell them they were kind to come and visit. If you do not feel up to anything more, you do not need to say anything other than "I'm feeling tired, so I need to rest."

If your stay in the hospital is a long one, you may not receive as many cards, flowers, telephone calls, or visits after awhile. People still care about you just as much, but they need to live their own lives, too. It can be hard for friends to watch you undergo treatment. Some people may even be afraid to come and see you. Just remember that people can react in a lot of different ways to having someone they care about in the hospital.

Also remember that your stay in the hospital is the best thing for you and your body. Make it your mission to make your stay as short as possible by keeping a positive attitude and being active in the process of healing. If you have enough energy to walk around the floor, go ahead and do so. Ask someone to come with you. Your doctor can recommend exercises, such as leg and arm lifts, that you can do in bed to keep your body from getting too far out of shape. Exercise will also help your appetite and your state of mind, and it is a major stress reliever. So if you can move, then move.

Try not to be a passive victim of cancer and your treatment. Be an active soldier. This is your time to focus on yourself and your health. If you need to eat pizza with pineapple and ham at four in the morning, and then you feel like taking a walk around the floor, do it. Stay as active as possible in mind and body.

How Others Respond to Your Cancer

When you first learned that you had cancer, you were probably immediately aware of two things: your emotional response to the news and the response of your family and friends. Your parents and your siblings, if you have any, will be very disturbed by your illness. Each parent and each brother or sister will react differently. And how they react can be stressful for you. After all, you care very much about them; you do not like to see them worried or sad. Even so, you cannot be responsible for your family's reaction to your illness. Having to cope with your own emotions is enough of a job right now. There are ways to make your family's response to your illness as stress-free as possible.

Parents

Whether it is your parents or another guardian, the people who take care of you love you very much. They want the best treatment for you. They may even argue with each other about what is best for you. Meanwhile, you are left without their support as they argue back and forth. Ask them not to argue in front of you because you need as much positive energy around you as possible.

Your parents want to help you, but they probably feel very helpless. A parent's first reaction is often to try to fix things for his or her child. Whether it was your mom who put a bandage on your scraped knee or your dad who fixed the bike that was damaged when you fell and cut that knee, your parents have been responsible for setting things straight.

Well, now they are faced with a situation that they cannot fix. No one can "fix" cancer. The stress they feel as a result of this can express itself in a number of different ways. They may fight with each other. They may become extremely overprotective and try to make every decision for you, from what you should eat to what you should be doing. They may try to restrict your activities or keep your friends from visiting, out of the fear that you will get tired out or exposed to new germs.

No matter how your parents react, the best way for you to deal with them is to be as honest as you can possibly be. Try to tell them what you need them to do for you. If they have specific things that they can do for you, they will feel less helpless and more in control. They will not have as much time to argue or worry about what you want from them. They want to give you support. If you need more hugs from them, ask for them. If you need space and time to be alone or talk with friends, ask for it.

Remember that your parents have feelings too. Respect their need to help you and feel like they have even a little bit of control over the situation. Ask them to be present with you during meetings with your doctors. Ask them to read up on your treatment so they can better understand what you are going through and help you make decisions if needed. Even if they have already set up camp in your room and read an entire library about cancer and its treatment, they need to know that you still depend on them for support.

Be aware, also, that your parents have yet another source of concern—money; specifically, how they are going to pay for your treatment. It can be very difficult for teens to understand just how stressful financial concerns can be for adults. You should not spend much time or energy worrying about this. You should not be spending your time and energy on anything except getting healthy. It will help you to understand your parents' reactions, however, if you recognize that they are dealing with very stressful concerns of their own.

Brothers and Sisters

Your siblings have shared things with you their whole lives—toys, potato chips, the phone, the television. They may not always feel as generous when it comes to sharing the attention of your parents to the extent that it may be necessary while you have cancer.

Quite naturally, while you are ill you are going to become your parents' number one concern. Your brothers and sisters may resent the attention and the money being spent on you and your treatment. This does not mean that they do not care about you. It is hard for kids and even young adults when their parents are forced to give them less attention. Your siblings may find themselves having to put up with a lot of baby-sitters, microwave dinners, and missed vacations so that your parents can take care of you.

There is no need for you to feel guilty, though. It is not your fault that you are sick. Your siblings might want to hear you say that you are sorry that you are taking so much of your parents' time, but you should not feel like you have to say anything. Like your parents, your siblings may feel powerless to help you. They may not know what to say to you or how to treat you. If you want, try to include your brothers and sisters in the relaxing activities that keep you busy during hospital stays or at home.

Sometimes it may seem like there is just no way to fix your relationship with your family. This is a hard time for everyone, so try to take it easy. Just do what feels natural. There are other options that you and your family may want to consider. If you think that you and your family would benefit from getting together and talking, you may want to consider working with a family therapist. Therapists are trained in enabling people to find productive ways to communicate with each other, particularly about difficult or painful topics or during stressful times.

You or other members of your family also might find group therapy productive. There are support groups specifically designed for the family of cancer patients. Many families have found such programs to be extremely helpful. It can be frustrating to get all your support and advice from doctors, nurses, and therapists who have never actually been in the situation you and your family are experiencing. Support groups create an arena in which family members can express all of the different things that they are feeling, hear about the similar experiences of others in the same situation, and receive advice and support from a caring group of people who are likely to have very similar experiences to draw from.

The thing to remember is that your family loves you and wants the best for you. Your parents may fight with each other. Your siblings may be giving you attitude. But you need to keep in mind that they are going through a lot of stress themselves. They have to watch someone they love—you—go through a very painful and difficult process, and they feel powerless to make it better. Remember that sometimes they may be overwhelmed by their own frustration at not being able to help. Seek support from therapy or other sources if necessary. Be honest and open with your family, and you all may be able to grow together as you face this challenge.

Friends, School, and Your Illness

Your friends may have a different reaction to your cancer. Each of them may respond differently, and the way they feel and respond may change over time. Some of your friends might treat you normally, as if everything was just fine. Others may treat you like a sick person. They may feel sorry for you or express their pity. They even may distance themselves from you.

All this can become even more complicated for them because you may want different things from them at different times. Sometimes you may need someone to feel sorry for you or express his or her sympathy. At other times, you may want your friends to treat you like absolutely nothing is wrong. Most often, you will want something in between. But remember, just as you might find it difficult to know exactly how you want to be treated, it can be equally difficult for friends to find that same balance.

It is not your responsibility to help your friends through whatever difficulty they might be having with your illness. Even so, it might help if you understand why they are behaving the way they are. Now that you are sick, you have a new perspective on things, but you may want to ask yourself if you would have known how to behave if the situation was reversed. Learning that a friend has such a serious illness can be very depressing. Seeing someone your own age so sick can also be extremely frightening. Your illness may be the first time that your friends have ever had to consider realistically the possibility of being very ill.

So how do you get the friendship and support you need from your friends? If they are your friends, then they want to help you. They may not know how to do that. So talk to them as honestly as you can about what you are feeling and about what they could do for you that would help. It does not have to be a big speech. Just tell them, "Hey, it's okay to be scared. I sure am, but I need you to just hang with me and watch *Dawson's Creek* or the World Cup, like we normally would." Or, "Listen, you have been kind of distant since I got cancer. I am angry that you would choose now to leave me without your friendship, since I really need you around. I understand how this can be hard for you, like maybe you don't know what to say or how to act, but just be open with me. Don't walk away, because I need you to help me get through this, okay?"

In an ideal world, all of your friends would be strong enough and smart enough to give you exactly the amount and kind of support you need. But face it, everyone has insecurities and fears. Try to remember: they want to be able to help you, they just might not know how. Do not think that if a friend is not giving you exactly what you need, he or she does not care. Most likely, your friends are thinking of you, wishing they could do something to help, and feeling helpless.

If all goes well during your hospital stay, you will experience either a remission—a period when you experience no symptoms of cancer—or even a cure. In either case, after some time to regain your strength, you may be ready to return to school.

Because cancer and its treatment can be hard on your body, you may look very different. You need to be prepared for the way people react to your changed appearance. Maybe you have shaved your head because of the hair loss from chemotherapy, or maybe you are wearing a wig. You may have lost a lot of weight or become swollen with water weight, which can be a side effect of cancer treatment. You may have scars that are visible to others.

Before you return to school, you should ask yourself if you feel ready to handle seeing—and being seen by—all your old classmates. People may be curious and want to ask you about your scar or how it is to have a shaved head, but they may feel embarrassed and not want to make you sad or angry. One way to deal with this is by breaking the tension yourself. A good way of doing this is by being open about acknowledging the ways that you have changed. Talk to your friends about it. Let a close friend touch your shaved head; it feels pretty cool. Show your close friends the scar on your stomach; they will probably be impressed by your strength.

Once people know that you are still comfortable with yourself, they will stop paying attention to those superficial markers of your challenges with cancer. They will again see you for who you are, and your scar or wig is not going to make any more difference than the color of your eyes.

Some people, possibly even some of your friends, may not know much about cancer. Believe it or not, some people may think it is contagious. This may make you angry, but remember that they are just scared. Let them know that it is okay, that cancer is not contagious. If they ask too many questions for you to answer, feel free to let them know that your school library has books about cancer, like this one, that can tell them all they want to know.

You may find yourself receiving attention from people who were never that close to you before. Try not to resent it. When young people see someone their own age get sick, it may really affect them. They may want to reach out to you for a number of reasons. Just try to accept any friendly action and thank them for their concern.

After your first few days back, you may find that you need to make an effort to get back into the swing of things. Your friends may go out of their way to include you in activities and conversations, but they may not. They may assume that you are tired or not ready to go out yet. If you do feel up to going out, tell your buddies. Initiate plans yourself for Friday night. Show up to parties with a smiling face, and before long your friends will be calling, gossiping, and hanging with you just like before.

Your schoolwork may have piled up while you were sick, but your teachers are sure to give you extensions and help you. You may need to make up work over the summer, and in the worst case, you may have to repeat a year. This may seem like a big deal, and it is—for now. But if cancer teaches you anything, it will be about the importance of your health. And once you have regained that, you will have plenty of time and opportunity to catch up with your schoolwork, learn all you want and need to know, and become whatever you want to be.

You may even find that your struggle with cancer has given you new strength and motivation to work really hard once you are feeling well again. You may find that you have a more positive attitude about school. Try to not let yourself get down about schoolwork. Talk to the school counselor or to a teacher you like if you need more support. You may not have a problem at all swinging back into academic life. But take things slowly, and do not expect to have enough energy right away to hang out with your friends, play all the sports you enjoy, do all your classwork, and participate in all your old activities. You may need to choose a few things to cut out of your list of obligations.

Chris

At sixteen, Chris was diagnosed with a malignant melanoma on the back of his thigh. Cancer cells were also found in a couple of lymph nodes, meaning that the cancer had begun to spread. He was treated with interferon injections, which he received until he graduated from high school at the age of eighteen.

Graduating on time was a major achievement for Chris, since the treatment left him feeling ill and tired much of the time. In order to graduate, he had to decide which of his activities were the most important to him, since he did not have enough energy to do them all. Though he missed the sport, he decided to stop playing on the basketball team. Since he sometimes had trouble keeping up with homework because he was tired a lot of the time, he also gave up writing the sports column for the school paper.

Chris definitely missed those activities, but he decided that having enough energy to attend school and keep up with his classwork, even while undergoing treatment, was more important. Being too busy while receiving his cancer treatment would have put Chris at risk of getting overwhelmed. His health could have suffered, as well as his performance in school. Now Chris has finished his treatment, is cancer free, and is attending college, where he is doing very well in all of his classes. All in all, he feels the decisions he made were the right ones.

None of this is meant to suggest that coping with melanoma is not one of the most difficult things that you will ever have to do. And finding the support that you need can feel like just another source of stress. There are a number of organizations that exist solely to help people, like you, in their battle with cancer. At the back of this book you will find the names, addresses, phone numbers, and Web sites of organizations that you might find helpful.

Healthy in Body and Mind

It is essential to remember that your mental health is a factor in your healing process. Cancer is a physical illness, but emotional well-being can help you achieve physical health.

You may think that when things get tough you are supposed to raise your chin up high, put on a stiff upper lip, and brave the storm alone and without complaint. Well, this can be a very unhealthy approach to difficult times. If you have cancer, you are experiencing what is likely to be the most difficult part of your life. Do not be ashamed if you want and need support from others. Unfortunately, you may feel like no one understands what you are going through, so how the heck is anyone supposed to give you support?

Your parents are definitely there to love you and care for you, but they are going through a difficult time themselves. You may not feel that you can ask them to help you vent your anger and sadness. The same may be true of brothers and sisters and friends. So where do you go? Who can you talk to about it? Who will listen and provide support?

Getting Support

Believe it or not, there is a whole group of people who do understand what you are going through—other cancer patients. You might try to keep in touch with the people you meet in the hospital or clinic where you receive treatment. They will probably be able to help you by listening and possibly even telling you their own stories about how they deal with cancer. It can be helpful for you and for other patients to be able to tell your stories and hear about the experiences of others.

Telling Your Story

By talking about your struggle, your achievements, and even your pain, you will be able to unload some of those painful emotions. They will no longer be trapped inside, making you even more stressed out. Other cancer patients will understand. They will be able to say, "Yeah, I know how tough that can be." They will know how amazing and impressive your achievements in your healing process have been. They will be able to give you advice or tips on how to improve your daily life while you struggle with cancer.

Listening to the Stories of Others

The act of listening to other people's stories can also be very helpful for you. You will find out that you are not as alone as you think in your struggle with your illness. Others have to deal with the same kinds of challenges, and others have struggled with them successfully. No one's story will be exactly like yours, that is true. Your sadness and pain are entirely yours and totally unique, but other people with cancer have been through similar things. You will learn that there are indeed many people who understand what you are going through, just as you are able to understand what they are going through and give them help and support.

So how do you get in touch with other people struggling with cancer? You may not be able to contact the patients you met in the hospital. Or maybe you were not really able to connect with anyone while you were receiving treatment.

Both of these are common experiences. Because patients and doctors have come to understand how much strength cancer patients gain by supporting each other, support groups have been formed to help cancer patients meet people who have gone through similar experiences. You may want to join a support group made up of people your age who have cancer and are dealing with the same issues. The hospital or clinic where you received your treatment should be able to refer you to the support groups in your area. Also, at the back of this book, there is a list of a few of the many organizations that work to make it easier for cancer patients and survivors to get in touch with each other for support.

Psychotherapy

Though it may be hard to believe, some people still think that psychotherapy is only for people who are "disturbed," or mentally ill. Although support groups are very helpful, you may find it hard to "open up" in a group setting. You may want more attention paid to your own personal issues, such as dealing with family and friends or your self-esteem.

If so, you may want to consider the option of talking to your own therapist. Shrinks are not just for crazy people. People talk to psychologists, psychiatrists, or therapists for millions of different reasons. You certainly have a valid reason to want to talk to someone who will help you process all the emotions you will have experienced since learning that you have cancer.

A therapist will help you to understand that it is healthier for you to face your emotions and learn to understand them rather than "deal" with them by always holding back and acting as if you always feel strong. Accepting your emotions requires more strength than pushing them aside. You need as much strength and self-understanding as you can achieve. It might be very helpful for you to have your own therapist to help you understand and process your feelings and the experience you are going through. If you still think that working with a therapist makes you "strange" or "weak," try to think of it instead as one more thing that you need to do to recover from cancer. There is nothing strange about wanting to get better.

Again, your doctors may be able to refer you to a therapist in your community who specializes in working with people who have cancer. Remember that not every therapist is right for everyone. Choose a therapist with whom you are comfortable. It may take a few appointments with different people until you "click" or "connect" with someone.

Eat, Sleep, and Play

It is a proven fact that stress can reduce the power of your immune system. Well, that's just great, right? Here you

99

are feeling rotten and totally stressed about the treatment, your friends, your family, school, or a hundred other things, and now you find out that all this stress is actually making it harder for your body to fight off the cancer.

Don't worry so much. There are many ways to reduce your level of stress and attain a more positive attitude about your situation. The best advice for doing so is to eat, sleep, and play. Each of these allows you to relax and assist your body in its struggle to become totally healthy again.

Eat for Health

Eating well affects your body and your state of mind. Ask your doctors or a nutritionist how you can best feed your body and mind. Should you be eating a lot of small meals throughout the day? Should you be eating certain types of food? If your treatment is making it hard for you to eat at all, do not make a lot of rules about the way you are going to eat. Just eat whatever you want, whenever you can. The goal is to help your body attain health, so avoid junk food as much as possible. And whatever you do, stay away from alcohol and tobacco.

Sleep

Your body needs a lot of energy to fight off cancer cells and to rebuild healthy cells. Cancer cells also channel a lot of your body's energy into helping them proliferate. The healthy processes of your body, including those of your immune system, are left without much fuel.

So besides needing to eat well, you may need to sleep

more than you usually would. Don't fight it. If you are tired, then sleep. Pace yourself through the day. When you feel alert and well rested, have visitors or do home-work. If you start to feel tired, let yourself relax. Hanging out with visitors can be draining, so if you feel tired, ask them to come back another time. They will understand. If you feel like you are sleeping too many of your days away, try to reserve your energy by engaging in relaxing activities. That way you will not feel so tired all the time, and you can stay alert for longer periods at a time.

It may be difficult for you to have less energy than you are used to, but do not get down on yourself. You are going through a difficult time now. Your mind and body are working overtime to keep you as healthy and calm as possible. So let yourself sleep or rest if you feel drained; the fatigue you are feeling is your body's way of telling you that it needs something. Listen to it, the same way you would like your family and friends to listen to you when you tell them what you need. Sleep and rest are two of the best ways the body knows to heal itself.

The Rest Is Play

If you have energy, then by all means play, play, play. Try some of the fun, stress-relieving activities listed below. Maybe they will give you even more ideas about how to relieve stress through playing.

Exercise

So you say that you want to decrease your stress, have some fun, avoid boredom, and increase your body's ability to fight off cancer? Exercise certainly provides those benefits. You may be familiar with that calm feeling you get after a hard game on the soccer or football field. Or maybe the peace you feel on the bus on the way home from a swim meet.

Whether or not you have felt the stress release that exercise provides, be assured that exercise does indeed reduce stress. Physical activity gets certain chemicals, called endogenous endorphins, pumping through your system. These are the same kind of chemicals found in prescription pain killers and are also the chemicals responsible for the famous "runner's high."

Think about it. You have a huge supply of "happy molecules" for your pleasure inside your own body. They are all natural, legal, and free. All you need to do to get these molecules active in your system is get moving. Exercise lets you take advantage of your body's own ability to decrease pain and stress.

Playing softball, dancing, or throwing the lacrosse ball around not only reduces stress but keeps you busy. It can be very depressing and boring to sit around the house or your hospital room all day watching the television or flipping through the same magazines ten times. Getting active, whether you do some sit-ups in the recreation room at the hospital or go for a run around your neighborhood, can keep your mind and body busy. Try to arrange activities with others, such as walking with a friend or playing a game of pickup hoops down at the basketball courts near your house.

Exercise reduces stress and depression. It keeps you busy and having fun. Exercise tunes up your body. Cancer works to destroy your body's tissues and its immune system. Exercise can improve your prognosis by getting your body in better physical condition so it can respond to therapy more efficiently. Exercise also keeps your muscles, including your heart, from getting weak and smaller from disuse. Keeping active can also speed your recovery by encouraging your body to maintain tissue and joint strength.

Exercise is one of the best ways to play. It reduces stress, keeps your mind off negative things, and helps your body stay healthy while it fights off cancer. Exercising can also make you feel more in control of your life. Going through all these treatments and having all these decisions made for you by doctors and family can make you feel like you are losing your grip on your life. Scheduling an exercise routine gives you something to be in control of and to look forward to, something that makes you feel good and helps you get as healthy as possible. This can help you feel good about yourself and give you a positive attitude that is essential in the healing process. So get out and play!

One note of caution: When you feel that you are ready to start an exercise program, talk to your doctor first. He or she may have some advice and suggestions. You also want to make sure that you take it easy at first. Pace yourself. Your energy level will not be what it once was. You need to get your body back into shape slowly.

Begin by walking or throwing a Frisbee around, just to be doing something active and fun. If at any point you feel pain, shortness of breath, or any kind of weakness, stop immediately. As a general rule, take it slow and try to get someone to exercise with you, just to be safe and to have some company.

Your Inner Voice

Most people talk to themselves. They may not do it by talking out loud, but each and every one of us has an inner voice. Some people call the inner voice the conscience. Some people call it their subconscious or unconscious. Some might even refer to it as their spirit or soul.

What you call it is not really all that important. What is important is how you relate to what your inner voice expresses.

Each person deals with difficult situations differently. How you respond to any situation, even one as trivial as being embarrassed over tripping, can affect your happiness and stress level. Everyone has experienced embarrassment at some point. Maybe you did something clumsy or "stupid" in front of a group of people. Maybe you forgot a line in a play or told a classmate you had a crush on him or her and the person laughed.

Well, everyone responds differently to embarrassment. Some people have an inner voice that says, "You idiot. You are so stupid. I can't believe you did that. Better get out of here before they get cramps from laughing so hard." These people have very critical inner voices. They are hard on themselves and get angry with themselves pretty easily.

Some people have inner voices that respond to embarrassment quite differently. Maybe they say, "Nice one. Almost as clumsy as when you fell down the stairs at the dance like that girl in *Clueless*." But then they laugh with those around them and forget it ever happened. These people have inner voices that are not as harsh and judgmental. They allow themselves to make mistakes without getting too angry or upset about it.

The point is that your inner voice really affects your state of mind. It talks to you twenty-four hours a day, seven days a week, 365 days a year. It can be pretty depressing if your inner voice sounds like an enemy. Listen to how you talk to yourself. Try to be positive. Do not be so critical. If you find that you often beat up on yourself, try to be a little nicer. Be your own best friend.

Be kind to yourself and treat yourself as well as you can. Do not scold yourself with lots of "I should haves." If you want to do something, do it because you can, not because you "should." Think of a person, real or fictional, that inspires you: *Rocky*, Michael Jordan, Jewel. Keep that inspirational person in your mind. Remember how much positive energy it takes to get to the top, to fulfill your dreams.

You are facing a huge challenge right now, one as great as any of your heroes have ever faced. No, you are not trying to make it to the Olympics or win the MVP award or dance on Broadway, but you need to be positive and keep supporting yourself. It will not matter very much how supportive everyone around you may be if you keep saying things to yourself like, "I can't make it through this" or "There's no way I can do that." Be your own cheering section. Pretend your inner voice is a really loud fan who keeps yelling, "You can do this! You're going to win this one!"

Write It Down

You may be overwhelmed by your feelings right now. It may seem like you just cannot get them all out. Maybe you feel like no one is listening to you or paying enough attention to you. Writing things down in a journal is another helpful way of expressing your thoughts and feelings.

105

Try to write something everyday, even if you feel like you do not have anything in particular to say. Draw something, or try to describe an unusual dream that you had. It is not important that you write deep and profound things or come away from your journal feeling like you have solved all the day's problems. Keeping a journal helps you stay in contact with your feelings and thoughts so that they do not build up and come out in destructive ways, such as anger or anxiety.

Hobbies

Things can change quite a bit once you are diagnosed with cancer. You may not be able to take part in all of the activities that you used to enjoy. Even so, you need to keep busy and find a way to express your creative energy. Therapists use art and other hobbies to help people learn how to deal with stress and other problems. Below are some hobbies and activities that people have found useful in dealing with stress.

- Cooking, especially for friends or other people

- Knitting or embroidering

- Wood carving

- Painting

- Drawing

- Playing a musical instrument

- Collecting—rocks, dried flowers, stamps, coins, or whatever interests you

⇨ Making centerpieces for holidays for your friends from flowers, vines, pinecones

⇨ Building or woodworking

⇨ Gardening

⇨ Refinishing furniture

⇨ Sewing

⇨ Playing computer games

Let Others Help

In a very helpful book called *I Can Cope: Staying Healthy with Cancer,* the authors suggest that cancer patients "eliminate Superman or Superwoman" from their lives. It is a very good idea. You need to realize that you will not be able to do everything you want to do on your own. If you need help getting things done—whether that means homework, cleaning your room, or with extracurricular activities—ask for it. You will probably find that others will be more than willing to give you a hand. In fact, by asking for help, you allow those who are close to you to feel like there is something specific that they can do to help you heal.

Meditation

Too far out, too spiritual or weird for you? Give it a chance. Meditation can be very relaxing and is an excellent way to achieve peace and quiet when you feel like things are spinning out of control.

You need four things to meditate: a quiet place; a comfortable, upright position; a clear mind; and a mantra. Once you have found a place where others will not bother you and you are seated comfortably, you need to put your mind in neutral. This can be very difficult and takes practice, so do not get frustrated if you cannot do it even after several tries.

Try to keep all thoughts out of your mind and concentrate on your mantra. A mantra is a word or phrase that you repeat over and over in your mind. It will become like a soothing song that guides you to a deep level of relaxation. You want to choose a short word or phrase that does not have any great emotional meaning for you. Try the word "one" as your mantra if you cannot think of your own.

Meditation is a skill and an art. It takes practice, just like any other skill, but it's worth it. But it is always worth the time, even if you never feel like you will be a pro at it. Just taking the time to be alone in a quiet and safe environment can be very beneficial to your well-being. Some books on meditation and other relaxation techniques are listed in the For Further Reading section at the back of the book.

Acupressure

Acupressure is another proven method of gaining relief from pain and stress. It is derived from acupuncture, which is an ancient Chinese technique for healing and pain relief.

There are many books on acupressure that you can consult. The basic theory is that the body contains various "pressure points." For example, the cleft between the thumb and index finger is believed to be such a pressure point. When moderate amounts of pressure are applied to these points—by pressing on them, for example—a person experiences relief from pain or stress and may even feel an increased overall sense of well-being. So you might want to think about browsing through a few books on acupressure at the local bookstore or library.

Massage

Massage is more difficult to perform on your own than acupressure or meditation. It is also more expensive and works best if it is performed by a trained professional. Even so, a massage can be very relaxing and can make your body feel more invigorated and healthy.

There are many different types of massage. Some, such as the Swedish deep massage, are aimed at releasing built-up tension in specific muscle groups where such tension tends to gather, such as your shoulders, legs, or lower back. Other types of massage simply attempt to create a sense of physical and spiritual harmony. Virtually any type of massage will feel good and relax you quite a bit.

If you cannot go to a professional masseuse, ask a friend or family member to give you a little massage. Any human touch, especially when needles and other medical devices are not used, is soothing to the spirit. Ask for whatever cuddling and contact you need. You will feel better, and so will those who care for you.

Imaging

Imaging will be most useful to you if you already have developed some skill at meditation. You do not need to be a meditation master; you just need to be able to get yourself into a very relaxed state of mind.

Once you have achieved this relaxed state, imagine yourself in a very comforting place. You can think of a real place that has always brought you a sense of peace or you can create an imaginary one for yourself. Maybe you are floating on a raft on a lake in the warm, summer sun. Maybe you are drifting on a cloud or lying on the grass in a spring meadow. You can explore as many different visualizations as you want. Use the ones that bring you the most happiness and contentment. As with meditation, there are many books about visualization or imaging that you can look at.

So eat, sleep, and play is the best recipe for stress reduction. Reduce the uncertainty you feel about your situation by learning all that you can about cancer, its treatment, and your overall physical and emotional well-being. Uncertainty causes stress. So the more you know, the less you will be unsure of, and the less stress you will feel. Do not worry too much about those things in your future that you cannot control. The best way to take care of tomorrow is to take care of yourself today.

Hope

Living with a chronic and possibly terminal illness is a huge challenge to the spirit. Take advantage of the many supportive people and organizations out there. Think of your cancer as a challenge, not an end. You are living with cancer, not dying of it. Be aware of how your inner voice represents your situation, and make that inner voice speak to you as positively as possible. Be as optimistic as you can.

Anger, fear, and loneliness are all normal emotions for someone who is coping with melanoma. Allow yourself to accept these emotions instead of putting on a stiff upper lip and pretending that you are just fine.

You are not coping with melanoma all by yourself. There are many other people fighting cancer who can relate to your suffering and your accomplishments. There are people who care about you. Work to build a supportive network of people with whom you can share your emotions.

The fight against melanoma is also going on in laboratories and clinics all around the world. Hundreds of physicians and scientists have devoted their careers to finding a cure for melanoma. Incredible advances in the treatment of melanoma are being made, with vaccine trails and gene therapy being two examples. Many people in the medical profession believe that melanoma will be the first cancer for which a cure will be found.

In the long run, there isn't anything that anyone else can say to you that will bring you the sense of optimism and calmness that you need in order to cope with melanoma. You must find that within yourself. A positive attitude—hope, in short—is the best weapon anyone has to conquer cancer.

Glossary

acral   Term used to describe a specific kind of melanoma that is usually found on the palms of the hands or the soles of the feet.

atypical nevus   A nevus that differs from the common types, displaying certain characteristics—changes in color, size, shape, and texture—that may indicate the beginnings of cancer.

basal cell   Cell of the innermost layer of the epidermis.

basement membrane   Structural layer of the skin on which the epidermis rests.

benign   Something that does not threaten life or health; used to describe a harmless tumor.

biopsy   The removal and examination of tissue, cells, or fluids from a living body.

cancer   A malignant tumor of potentially unlimited growth that can spread to other parts of the body through a process known as metastasis.

carcinogenic   Causing or contributing to the development of cancer.

carcinoma   A malignant tumor that originates in the epithelium.

chronic   A condition that is characterized by long duration and frequent recurrence.

clear margins   Term used by physicians to indicate when there is no remaining lesion tissue after an excision biopsy.

cryotherapy   Treatment of a lesion by freezing it.

dermatologist   A doctor who specializes in treatment of the skin.

dermis   Innermost layer of the skin; it is made up of fibers and immune system cells and contains the nerve and blood supply the skin needs.

diagnosis   Identification of a disease or medical condition by its signs and symptoms.

electron microscope   Type of microscope that allows pathologists to examine cells in extreme detail, down to their atomic structure.

epidermis   Outermost layer of the skin; the part of the skin that you can see and touch. The epidermis is itself made up of several layers of cells.

excision biopsy   Surgical removal of an entire lesion for the purpose of diagnosis.

freckle   Flat, tan spots on the skin caused by melanocytes in that area overproducing melanin.

frequency   Rate with which a disease occurs within a specified number of the population.

granular cell   Skin cell of the layer of the epidermis where the skin cell's DNA begins to disintegrate.

hypothesis   In science or medicine, a theory or explanation that can be verified or refuted by experiment, analysis, and observation.

immunocytochemistry   Diagnostic technique used by pathologists that involves the adhesion of a specific protein to certain cells.

incidence   Rate of occurrence.

incisional biopsy   Removal of only a part of a lesion for pathological examination.

intermittent   Varying in frequency or occurrence.

keratin   A protein that is common in the skin.

keratinocyte   The most common type of skin cell.

Langerhans cell   Cell of the epidermis involved in the body's immune defense responses.

lentigo   Heavily pigmented areas of skin, resembling freckles, but larger and permanent.

macular   Spotted or blotched.

malignancy   The quality or state of being malignant.

malignant Something that threatens life or health; when said of a tumor, it means the tumor is of a kind that tends to invade other parts of the body, metastasize, and often end in death.

melanin Skin pigment.

melanocyte An epidermal cell that produces melanin.

melanoma A tumor, usually malignant, that contains dark pigment.

negligible Of no statistical or medical importance.

nevus A pigmented area on the skin; commonly referred to as a birthmark or mole. A birthmark is a congenital nevus.

nodular Of or pertaining to nodes.

nodule A small, raised growth on the skin.

prognosis Likelihood of recovery from a disease or medical condition.

radiation Energy emitted in the form of waves or particles.

solar Of or pertaining to the sun.

spindle cell Skin cells of the spindle layer of the epidermis; so called because they look as if they have spines or spindles.

squamous cell Skin cell of the outermost layer of the epidermis.

ultraviolet (UV) radiation A type of radiation that has a wavelength shorter than wavelengths of visible light; for most people, the sun is the leading source of UV radiation.

Where to Go for Help

American Academy of Dermatology
A national organization of the doctors who diagnose and treat skin problems. It provides a doctor referral service and free booklets on skin cancer.
P.O. Box 4014
930 North Meachum Road
Schaumburg, IL 60168-4014
(703) 330-0230

American Cancer Society (ACS)
A national organization that operates educational programs and provides support services. To get in touch with your local ACS, contact the national office.
1599 Clifton Road NE
Atlanta, GA 30329
(800) ACS-2345

Cancer Care, Inc.
A nonprofit organization which provides professional counseling, support, education, and telephone services to cancer patients and their families. It can also get you in touch with other patients and families so you can get support from others who are going through similar experiences.
1180 Avenue of the Americas
New York, NY 10036
e-mail: info@cancercareinc.org
Web site: http://www.cancercareinc.org
Cancer Care Counseling Line: (800) 813-HOPE

Candlelighters Childhood Foundation, Inc.
An international organization of parents of children who have or have had cancer. The foundation provides guidance, emotional support, and referral services through self-help and support groups. There are adolescent support groups, a youth newsletter, and the foundation even provides practical support via crisis intervention, baby-sitting, and transportation.
7910 Woodmont Avenue, Suite 460
Bethesda, MD 20814
(800) 366-2223

Crossing Bridges
A very helpful support network provided for interferon therapy cancer patients by the company that makes Intron A, the interferon injection. It provides educational literature, nurse counselors, and several support networks. Its Buddy Program will pair you with a former Intron A injection patient who will help you get through the therapy. Its Coach Program helps guide a caregiver to provide you with the best support possible.
Intake Initiatives Inc
185 Berry Street, Suite 4805
San Francisco, CA 94107-9412
(888) 77-BRIDGE /(888) 772-7434
Fax: (800) 683-7855

Kaplan Comprehensive Cancer Center Information and Treatment Service (CITS)
A telephone service by which information on clinical trials can be obtained.
NYU Medical Center
550 First Avenue
New York, NY 10016
9am-5pm, Monday-Friday
(212) 263-6485

116

Make-a-Wish Foundation
An organization that works with families of terminally ill children under the age of eighteen. It provides the financial assistance and arrangements necessary to grant a child's special wish, such as meeting a favorite role model.
100 West Clarendon, Suite 2200
Phoenix, AZ 85013-3518
(602) 279 9474

National Cancer Institute (NCI)
Cancer Information Service is a nationwide telephone service provided by the National Cancer Institute (NCI). The staff who answer the phones can answer questions, send booklets on skin cancer, and refer you to the resources and services in your area. There are both English and Spanish-speaking staff members. NCI booklets: *Good News, Better News, Best News: Cancer Prevention, What You Need to Know About Melanoma,* and *What You Need to Know About Skin Cancer*
Office of Cancer Communications
Bethesda, MD 20205
(800) 4-CANCER / (800) 422-6237

Skin Cancer Foundation
Provides educational materials and also publishes *Sun and Skin News* and *The Skin Cancer Foundation Journal.* These two journals have nontechnical articles on skin cancer in order to promote public knowledge. You can receive free information if you send the headquarters a stamped, self-addressed envelope.
Suite 2402
245 Fifth Avenue
New York, NY 10016
(212)-725-5176

For Further Reading

Anderson, G. *The Cancer Conquerer.* New York:
    Plume/Penguin, 1991.

—— *50 Essential Things to Do When the Doctor Says It's
    Cancer.* New York: Plume/Penguin, 1993.

Benson, H., and M.Z. Klipper. *The Relaxation Response.* New
    York: Avon, 1976.

Carty, Amy. *Positive Visualizations For People with Cancer
    and Those Who Love Them.* Boston: Birchard Books,
    1992.

Grealy, L. *Autobiography of a Face.* New York:
    HarperPerrennial, 1995.

Hanpham, W.S., M.D. *After Cancer: A Guide to Your New
    Life.* New York: HarperPerrennial, 1995.

—— *Diagnosis Cancer: Your Guide Through the First Few
    Months.* New York: Norton, 1998.

Hoek, B.H. *Cancer Lives at Our House: Help for the Family.*
    Detroit: Baker Books, 1997.

Johnson, J., and Klein, L. *I Can Cope: Staying Healthy with
    Cancer.* Minneapolis: Chronimed Publishing, 1994.

LeVert, S. *When Someone You Love Has Cancer.* New York:
    Dell, 1995.

Poole, C. *Melanoma Prevention, Detection, & Treatment.* New
    Haven: Yale University Press, 1998.

Yount, L. *Cancer.* San Francisco: Lucent Books, 1991.

Journals

Coping Magazine
2019 North Carothers
Franklin, TN 37064
(615) 790-2400

Sun and Skin News:The Skin Cancer Foundation Journal
Skin Cancer Foundation
Suite 2402
245 Fifth Avenue
New York, NY 10016
(212) 725-5176

Surviving!
Stanford University Medical Center
Patient Research Center, Room H0103
Division of Radiation Oncology
300 Pasteur Drive
Stanford, CA 94305
(415) 723-7881

Index